Sewing with Fabulous Vintage Fabrics

Sewing with Fabulous Vintage Fabrics

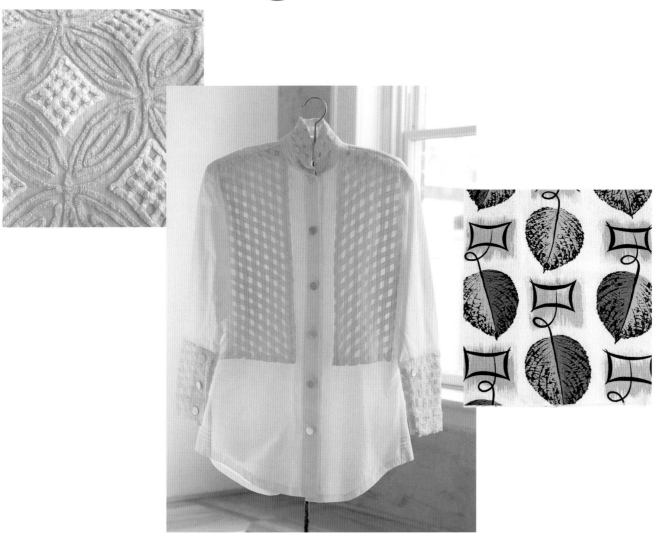

Arden Franklin

LARK BOOKS

A Division of Sterling Publishing Co., Inc.
New York

Editor: Valerie Van Arsdale Shrader
Art Directors: Susan McBride and Kathleen Holmes
Photographer: Sandra Stambaugh
Cover Designer: Barbara Zaretsky
Illustrator: Jennifer D. Wallace
Associate Art Director: Shannon Yokeley
Editorial Assistance: Delores Gosnell, Jeff Hamilton, Rebecca Lim

Library of Congress Cataloging-in-Publication Data

Franklin, Arden.
    Sewing with fabulous vintage fabrics by Arden Franklin.-- 1st ed.
        p.   cm.
    Includes index.
    ISBN 1-57990-457-2 (hardcover)
    1. Sewing.   2. Dressmaking.   3. Recycling (Waste, etc.)   4. Household linens.
        I. Title.
    TT715.F8358 2004
    646.2--dc22   2003026269

10 9 8 7 6 5 4 3 2 1

First Edition
Published by Lark Books, a division of Sterling Publishing Co., Inc.
387 Park Avenue South, New York, N.Y. 10016

© 2004, Arden Franklin

Distributed in Canada by Sterling Publishing, c/o Canadian Manda Group,
One Atlantic Ave., Suite 105 Toronto, Ontario, Canada M6K 3E7

Distributed in the U.K. by Guild of Master Craftsman Publications Ltd., Castle Place, 166
High Street, Lewes, East Sussex, England BN7 1XU Tel: (+ 44) 1273 477374, Fax: (+ 44)
1273 478606, Email: pubs@thegmcgroup.com, Web: www.gmcpublications.com

Distributed in Australia by Capricorn Link (Australia) Pty Ltd., P.O. Box 704, Windsor,
NSW 2756 Australia

If you have questions or comments about this book, please contact:

Lark Books
67 Broadway
Asheville, NC 28801
(828) 253-0467

Manufactured in China

ISBN 1-57990-457-2

Dedication

This book is dedicated to
all women who crave a
creative outlet in their lives.
May this book help you
create one of your own.

Contents

Introduction

What does vintage mean to you? The word refers to something with lasting appeal, something that was the best and most distinctive of its kind. Fine linens and fabrics certainly meet this definition, with their delicate hand and beautiful embellishments such as lace and embroidery. I have always loved these elegant old linens. My grandmother, mother, and aunt each had a collection that I remember them using regularly, but I also remember the special care their linens required—the pressing, the starching, and the laundering. As life grew busier in the last century, it became impractical to use these kinds of linens everyday. They've been relegated to the dusty attic or the stuffed trunk, neglected by a generation that's constantly on the go.

But as a seamstress with an eye for beautiful fabric, I discovered that embellishing sewing projects with old textiles gives a new garment the enduring appeal that's the very definition of vintage. Working with fabric, patterns, and colors has always been a joy to me. I was hooked on sewing when I made my first dress in my eighth-grade home economics class. Later on, I was able to indulge my passion by working part-time at a local fabric shop, and eventually I became a dressmaker there. Working at that shop, Virginia's Designer Fabrics, expanded my creative horizons and taught me a lot about the numerous options inherent in every sewing project.

Eventually, I started incorporating vintage linens into some of the garments I made. I scavenged closets and attics and garage sales looking for beautiful linens with exceptional details. My love for these textiles led to my own cottage industry, designing and making garments and home accessories.

When I began to sew professionally, I discovered that making an heirloom dress from scratch—purchasing new laces and trims and piecing them together—was very expensive, not to mention time consuming. But the lovingly recycled pieces I began to use instead were made from fine fabrics, and the exquisite cutwork, drawnwork, specialty edging, and embroidery were already present. Furthermore, I found that the charming fabrics so popular in the middle of the last century were great to incorporate into sewing projects, too, so "vintage" can mean anything from the fancy and frilly to the fun and funky. Once I began to sew with vintage textiles, I found a creative outlet that I'm still exploring today.

I'm eager to share my secrets with you. I've included more than 30 projects for clothing and home décor, discussing the entire process from purchasing a textile and laying out the pattern pieces to constructing the item. Since you'll be using purchased patterns to construct many of these projects, I've given you all of the information you need to find them, as well as specific advice on sewing each item. You'll find lots of tips throughout the book to make the process easier and allow you to express your creativity when working with these precious linens and textiles. *Sewing with Fabulous Vintage Fabrics* begins with some important advice on working with vintage fabrics, followed by a step-by-step guide to sewing with these textiles. You'll find a

wide range of projects for
every liking—an exquisite
christening gown with antique
lace, a denim jacket with a
vintage fur collar, a lovely
linen pillow, or a jaunty set of
café curtains.

Please take the time to explore
the possibilities presented by
heirloom pieces that have the
distinctive and enduring
appeal that's the very essence
of vintage. Whether you've
just begun to sew or you're
an experienced seamstress, I hope
you'll be inspired to work with these cherished pieces
of our past. I believe you'll delight in these fabrics as much I do.

My ultimate goal is to help you think beyond the traditional boundaries
of sewing. Incorporating a lovely handkerchief, a beautiful dresser scarf,
or a delicate doily into your work adds a whole new level of creativity

because you design the look of the
piece as well as construct it. Yes, every
one of you has the potential to be a
designer! I promise to share all of my
knowledge with you, illustrating how
to use these special textiles that can
add so much character to our lives.

Vintage Fabric Basics

Learn about the special qualities of vintage textiles and glean some tips for sewing with these wonderful fabrics.

Before You Start

Sewing with Fabulous Vintage Fabrics is a practical guide to sewing with vintage textiles, teaching you how to use these linens and fabrics in new and exciting ways. Before I discuss the first step in the process—finding a vintage linen—here are three keys to a successful project. All of these ideas are demonstrated throughout the book.

Think in terms of individual elements, not the whole.

Imagine how you can use small pieces of vintage linens to accent portions of a garment or home accessory. For example, you may have a beautiful old nightgown with some exquisite latticework that you'd like to use, but the latticework is too small to make an entire garment. Consider using the latticework for the front overlay and cuffs of a gorgeous blouse, like the one shown at the left. Or, suppose you have a charming old napkin with perfect lace and embroidery. Consider cutting it into squares, repositioning the pieces, and using them as the top of a pillow. Look at this project on page 30.

Be creative with the placement of the project's pieces.

When you construct an entire garment from a vintage linen, such as a tablecloth, lay out each individual piece so the designs on the fabric will be displayed in the most pleasing way on the finished project. Look at the jacket at the top of page 11 to see how the lines of chenille become a design element in this garment. You can even alter the pattern pieces to suit the design of your textile. The projects in *Sewing with Fabulous Vintage Fabrics* contain dozens of tips to help you use your fine textiles most effectively, and to take advantage of all these

Use vintage textiles to emphasize individual elements in a project, like the overlay and cuffs in this blouse.

suggestions, look for the quick guide to tips and alterations on page 27. It references both helpful techniques and problem-solving ideas.

Use simple but stylish patterns that allow the fabrics to shine.

Some time ago, I made a basic dress for a family friend using an extraordinary lace fabric. It turned out beautifully, and I was later able to create an entirely different look from the very same dress, with only minor changes. That's when I realized that a pattern with simple styling can result in a stunning garment if it's combined with a gorgeous fabric. The darling quilted jacket on page 87 is a perfect example. With these techniques for incorporating vintage linens, you'll find that you can create designer looks for a fraction of the cost of a designer dress or home accessory. Similarly, using vintage fabrics in home décor projects gives them a unique, personalized look that engages your creativity in

Use the textile's design to your advantage. Note how the lines of chenille look like a band at the hem of this jacket.

the process.

Keep these three principles in mind as you plan a project, and you'll think of sewing in a new light. Expand the boundaries of the craft. Add your own design ideas as you incorporate these special fabrics into your work. And remember that you're also working with history when you sew.

Use simple construction for your projects. Then the emphasis is on the fabric itself, like the rich matelasse used in this project.

Finding Vintage Fabrics & Notions

Before you begin to sew, you need just the right piece of vintage fabric. The first place to look is your own attic, closet, or trunk. You probably have some items that have sentimental, but not practical, value that are perfect for transforming into something new. Perhaps you have some treasured family pieces you're longing to use. If you don't have any inherited linens or vintage textiles in your family, they're easily found at garage sales, flea markets, and antique malls. If your taste runs more to mid-century designs such as abstract or geometric prints, atomic designs, and bold colors, look to the Internet, vintage fabric stores, and second-hand shops for these gems from the 1940s and 1950s. Whatever your personal taste, you can use your creativity to bring these linens and fabrics to life again.

To enhance the authenticity of your garments, add vintage accouterments like exquisite buttons, luxurious ribbons, and dainty laces, which are also readily available at the sources listed above. I like to use mother-of-pearl buttons on all of my garments, and I've found lots of them at flea markets. Don't forget to use the Internet as a resource, as I've found linens and specialty buttons online. Lots of antique dealers have bits and pieces of lace, and I occasionally find silk ribbon (which is very expensive if you buy it new). Buttons and trims from the mid-century era are easy to find, too. Of course, any of these ribbons and laces can be cleaned, just like the linens.

This is a very special piece of mine, a handkerchief that a friend of my great-grandmother made for my mother's wedding. It's pictured here with the very thread she used. I don't plan to ever cut it unless I incorporate it into something precious to me, such as a wedding dress or christening gown.

Remember that many people have linens stored away, but not everyone is a seamstress with an imagination. Friends have generously offered me their linens when they realized I was going to put them to good use in a meaningful way, like making a christening gown. Even if the linens you find are stained and torn, they can sometimes be your best finds, as long as most of the material is still in good condition. In fact, I seek out these kinds of textiles because they're inexpensive and perfectly salvageable. Most stains can be easily removed with a little patience. You can make repairs to vintage linens, too; read more about stain removal and repair techniques on pages 16 and 17.

Since I'm confident I can remove most stains, and either repair or cut around holes, the only textiles that I avoid are those in which the fibers themselves are damaged and suffer from rot. These linens will feel brittle. To test the health of the fibers, pull the fabric gently; if the fibers break, it's too damaged to use.

When you're shopping for vintage fabrics, think about what kind of clothing or home accessory you might make. A bright floral cotton tablecloth makes a great summer vest or top. A cutwork tablecloth is perfect for a lined garment (and you can fully line anything). Don't limit your thinking to just one piece of fabric—think of combining several. You could use a floral tablecloth for a top, and make the collar from a plaid hand towel that matches one of the colors in the tablecloth. A coat or vest made from a chenille bedspread could be made resplendent with a collar and cuffs from your grandmother's old mink stole— you know, the one with the head and tail! I'll tell you how to remove those little appendages on page 67, and you'll have the makings of a truly special garment. Laces and decorative trims can be combined in the same project, too.

Sewing children's clothing offers lots of room for creativity. You can make beautiful dresses out of vintage linens that feature embroidery and lace and they'll be as pretty as the French handsewn dresses that take a lot more time *and* money. Using vintage fabrics for kids gives you the opportunity to be a little zany,

What's a Bridge Cloth?

Remember your mother cleaning the house for days to host her bridge club? You probably didn't pay much attention to the tables (just the candy dishes on them), but each was likely covered with a 36 x 36-inch square tablecloth that is now referred to as a bridge cloth. I've used many of them in the book, especially in the girls' dresses. The square size is standard.

This lovely dress was made from a well-used tablecloth, but the linen's lovely floral design and a coordinating bow made it special.

The exquisite tucks and lace at the hem of this christening gown were removed from a vintage petticoat. Look for these kinds of special details when you're searching for vintage textiles.

too: you can add silly buttons and use all sorts of crazy fabrics for pockets and collars and cuffs. (Those fun 1950s prints are perfect.)

Remember, too, that you'll learn how to work around the imperfections in your vintage pieces. Be creative when you're shopping, and don't restrict yourself to looking for only a tablecloth or a handkerchief. I've used sheer curtains, antique petticoats, dresser scarves, bedspreads, napkins, and table runners, among other things. I buy pieces that appeal to me, knowing I'll eventually find a project for them. Look for details like tucks and elaborate laces that are too time-consuming to make by hand; these will add character to your projects with very little work from you! Again, most of these linens can be purchased at very reasonable prices, especially those textiles suffering from overuse or neglect.

Using Vintage Fabrics

To help you begin thinking about sewing with vintage fabrics, here's a short guide to textiles, organized by size. I've included some suggested uses for each type.

LARGE TEXTILES

This category includes all tablecloths and sheets (the things you generally think of as linens), as well as bedspreads and quilts. They generally vary from lightweight to medium-weight. The variety of tablecloths is endless— sheer, boldly patterned, embroidered, embellished with cutwork—and you'll find them made of both linen and cotton. Luxurious 100 percent cotton and linen sheets are also available, usually in white or off-white. Chenille bedspreads and cutter quilts are great finds also.

Above is the original tablecloth, a large piece, and at the right is the skirt made from it.

The most important point about finding a large, intact linen is that it will usually give you enough fabric to make an entire garment. You can get a skirt and matching blouse for an adult out of a large tablecloth; even a small tablecloth will provide enough material for a child's dress or an adult vest. Pure linen and cotton sheets are great for nightgowns and robes because they feel so fabulous on the skin; if they have embroidery, you can incorporate it into your design. Cotton and linen sheeting is utilitarian and can be used for the body of dresses and for lining pieces, too. Bedspreads and cutter quilts are perfect for cozy jackets; sofa-cushion covers made from chenille are featured on page 82.

Shown above is the uncut, medium-size table runner; below is the market bag it became.

MEDIUM TEXTILES

Table runners, bridge cloths, dresser scarves, and place mats fall into this category, and you can often find lace pieces that are big enough to be considered a medium-sized linen. They can be large enough to make a child's dress or an entire pillow or purse. These items can also be used for collars, cuffs, sleeves, and yokes, or applied to the bottom of a child's dress.

SMALL TEXTILES

Handkerchiefs, hand towels, lace doilies, and small table linens like dinner or cocktail napkins fit in here. You can use these small pieces on the yokes and sleeves of children's clothes, on a collar or cuff of an adult garment, or as an embellishment for a pocket. A collage technique that incorporates scrap linens allows you to make wonderful, crazy quilt-style bags or other items like bookmarks that you'll see on page 35. I've actually made large pieces of fabric collage and given them to a professional upholsterer to use in covering a chair. Though a piece of fur isn't a textile, I'll put it in this category too, because it does make sumptuous cuffs and collars.

Look through the projects that begin on page 29 for more examples of how I've used these various vintage textiles, bed linens, and table linens. The Fabric Gallery on page 128 shows you what some of these fabrics looked like before they were incorporated into a project, and then offers a photo of the finished project, too.

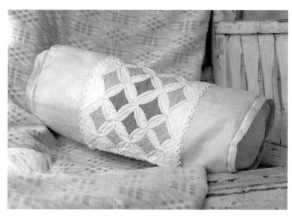

Above is the small dresser accessory; at the right, it's been transformed into a pillow.

Cleaning Vintage Textiles

Oftentimes, the pieces you find can use a little tender loving care, i.e., a good cleaning. The chemical compound sodium perborate, a mild oxidizing agent, is my best suggestion, but it's sometimes hard to find in its pure state. A drug store may be able to order a small quantity of sodium perborate for you, but it's least expensive when bought in bulk. Check the Internet or a swimming pool supply store for it, too.

Fortunately, you can also find products that contain sodium perborate in your grocery store, such as the powdered bleaches that are safe for colored clothing. There are also general-purpose stain removers than contain sodium perborate. If you can't find sodium perborate in its purest form, use one of these products. Be sure to check the label to see that the product contains sodium perborate—you may have to search the fine print to find the ingredients.

It's easy to cut around stains or holes when you're using a large tablecloth for a project such as this charming dress. You'll probably have plenty of useable material.

For cleaning and stain removal, soak the linens overnight in this solution: ½ cup of sodium perborate per gallon of warm water. (You'll need to use a larger quantity of the substitute products that contain sodium perborate.) If the stains don't come out to your satisfaction, try soaking them again in a fresh solution. After the stains have been removed, eliminate the chemical smell by washing the linens by hand or machine, using a mild detergent.

Repairing Vintage Textiles

You can approach tears or holes two ways: You can try to repair them, or you can cut around them. If you need to repair a small tear or hole that may be in a portion of the linen that you really want to use, set your machine on an embroidery (or tight zigzag) stitch and sew up the tear. Although small holes aren't really that noticeable, you don't want them to continue to ravel, so you should darn all holes with a tight zigzag stitch. Sometimes you can make the hole appear to be part of the fabric; for instance, if you find a hole in a vintage linen that features cutwork, embroider around it and the hole will look like part of the cutwork.

Since you're cutting the linens into pieces anyway, it's easy to circumvent stains, holes, and tears when cutting out your project. The collage technique I mentioned on page 15 is a great way to use small remnants of linens and lace. The tight zigzag keeps the remnants from raveling, just as it prevents a hole or tear from worsening.

Storing Textiles and Accessories

After I've cleaned and freshened my textiles, I always iron them before I store them. I use a water bottle to spritz the linens while I'm ironing. If I encounter some stubborn wrinkles, I take a damp cloth and place it on top of the wrinkled linen as I press.

As for storage, I have a metal bin with sliding drawers, but I also keep my vintage pieces in clear plastic bins and drawers so I can quickly survey what I have when I'm designing a garment. I store buttons in transparent plastic containers with dividers, sorted by size, and I keep ribbons and lace in clear plastic bags and place them in open bins, where I can see them. Archival-quality storage media is available if you'll be keeping fabrics and notions for some time before you use them in a project.

Will This Crochet Come Apart?

Don't be afraid to use vintage crochet. You might think it would unravel quickly, but it ravels only a little bit. After you cut the crocheted piece, zigzag the raw edge for stability.

Sewing with Vintage Fabrics

Now that you've found the perfect fabric, it's time to think about sewing. You can really approach this process from two different angles. You've found a garment or home accessory pattern you love, you want to make the item, and you'd like to find some marvelous fabric. Or, you've found some great vintage linens and want to make something equally wonderful from them. Either way, remember the main criterion in choosing a purchased pattern—it should have fairly simple construction that allows the fabric to be displayed in its full glory. For example, you may want to avoid a garment pattern with tucks, because the tucks would distort the design elements on the graphic tablecloth that you might use to make the garment. Study the purchased patterns I used to get a sense for which styles work well when you want to emphasize the design of the fabric. Although you'll make some custom patterns for the home décor projects in the book, I've used this same principle in designing these items—the simple styling focuses attention on the fabric, not the construction.

So, you've chosen a project and you've got the textiles you need. Here's an overview of how I prepare to sew, along with a few specialized tips for working with vintage fabrics. Yes, there are some basic sewing reminders, too.

Getting Ready to Sew

Before I use a new purchased pattern, I trace it and make a muslin.

TRACING A PURCHASED PATTERN

Since patterns today contain multiple sizes, I always make a copy of the pieces in my size and retain the original pattern intact. The best paper I've found for this step is lightweight tracing paper, which architects overlay on their drawings to illustrate changes to their designs. (You may find this paper called architectural "trash paper.") I also use it to make my own custom pattern pieces, as you'll see when you read through the project section that begins on page 29. You can buy tracing paper at drafting or architectural supply stores, as well as on the Internet, and a roll of it will last a *long* time. Be sure to get the 36-inch-wide roll.

I eliminated the tucks at the hem of this dress so the design elements in the tablecloth wouldn't be distorted.

Select the pattern pieces you'll use for your garment and place each piece under the tracing paper. Trace your size with a pencil and be sure to copy all the markings from the original pattern piece. Cut out the traced copy of each pattern piece, and when you're done, store them in a clear plastic bag, labeled with the size and pattern number for future reference.

MAKING A MUSLIN

This is a step that a lot of people would prefer to skip, but my dressmaker's experience shows me how valuable it is, so I suggest you take the time to do it. A muslin is a simple prototype of a garment with no facings or linings, and the name comes from the inexpensive fabric from which these prototypes are often made.

The making of a muslin gives you a good idea of how the final garment will be constructed. It also lets you know how the pattern pieces should be laid out, how the garment style looks on you, and whether it fits correctly. This step can actually save you a lot of time, money, and frustration in the long run, especially when using a precious, one-of-a-kind vintage linen.

To make muslins, I look for inexpensive lightweight or medium-weight fabric and buy it in bulk. When you construct your muslins, sew together only the basic garment pieces, omitting the facings or linings. Try on the garment to check the fit, remembering to account for the seam allowances.

It's rarely necessary to make a muslin for a home décor project, because you have exact measurements to use. It's easier to fit a chair than adapt a garment to a body whose dimensions may vary slightly from those in the pattern.

LAYING OUT YOUR PROJECT

After making a muslin, you'll have a complete understanding of the construction of your garment. Remember to think in terms of the individual elements—the collar, the cuffs, the yoke—as you study your vintage fabric.

This reversible wrap-around skirt used not one but two vintage textiles. Making a muslin insures you like the style and fit of a pattern before you cut any precious vintage textiles and use them in a project.

Do I Have Enough Fabric?

Since you're using a finite amount of vintage textile, you have to determine if you have enough fabric to make a whole garment or just some of the pieces. Although you can check the pattern envelopes for yardage requirements, the only true way to judge is to place the pattern pieces on the textile. If you don't have the necessary fabric to accommodate all of your pattern pieces, you can cut some of the pieces out of a coordinating fabric or use a different fabric for linings or facings, for instance.

For many of the home décor projects, you'll need to measure the item you're accessorizing and estimate how much fabric you'll need, making and placing a paper copy of the pieces on your vintage linen if necessary. Home décor projects often

take a lot of yardage, so consider using vintage pieces for highlights—the top of a cushion or a footstool cover—cut from chenille, barkcloth, or an old quilt, for example. Complete the project with purchased fabric that coordinates with your vintage piece.

An important point to make here is *you can't follow your purchased pattern's instructions for laying out the pieces,* because you may have more, or less, fabric than the instructions specify. Furthermore, to best utilize your vintage fabric, you may need to fold the fabric crosswise, rather than lengthwise, which is generally suggested in purchased pattern directions. Or, you might have to fold the fabric again after cutting out the first few pieces. For each project in this book, I've included a layout sketch. While your vintage textile may not be exactly the same size as the one I used or have the same design, you should be able to transfer my concept to your project. Look at how I laid out the individual pieces to take best advantage of the design of the fabric.

Lay out the pattern pieces to incorporate the textile's unique design elements, like the rows of cross-stitch on this tablecloth.

When you're placing the pattern pieces, pay attention to how the fabric's design is displayed on each element. If you have rows of embroidery on a tablecloth, arrange the pattern pieces so the embroidery flows down the front and the back of the garment. If you're using a cotton tablecloth with clusters of flowers or fruit, place them in the center of the front, the back, and the sleeves. Be sure the layout has visual appeal.

If a tablecloth has a pretty edge, you can use it as the hemline, omitting a standard hem, or use it as the bottom edge of a sleeve. Center the pieces of your pattern over embroidered designs or cutwork to emphasize these decorative features. If your textile has stripes, remember to match them just as you would if you were using a regular fabric. To make the best use of your vintage linen, you may have to cut the pieces out individually.

Although I've been primarily addressing garment construction in this section, the same rules apply to laying out the pieces of a home décor project. Whether you use a purchased pattern or make your own custom pattern pieces, display the textile's design to the best advantage of your project.

This part of the process is fun and allows you complete creative control over the final appearance of the project. Play with the placement of the pattern pieces during this stage, being mindful of the design of the fabric and the project you're making. Be imaginative and change the layout until you're satisfied you've found the best placement.

This blouse, made from a beautiful embroidered curtain, uses the scalloped edging of the curtains at the cuffs and the edge of the overlay.

Constructing Your Garment or Home Accessory

Now it's time to start the construction of your project. Here's a brief discussion of construction, followed by some tips about working specifically with vintage linens. Of course, the rules of good sewing apply to all of these projects.

CONSTRUCTION BASICS

A garment may have as few as two pieces, like the vest shown below. Usually, the more pieces in a purchased pattern, the more difficult and time consuming it is. As I said before, I prefer to use simple patterns with design flair rather than work with complicated ones. It's the material you choose that makes a simple garment very special, and these special textiles are what this book is all about. This is especially true when working with old linens that already have elegant embellishment like handwork or cutwork. Someone else has already done the hard work of making these beautiful pieces so you don't have to!

An upper-body garment must always have a front and a back. Sometimes it may have a front or back yoke, side panels, a collar, and/or sleeves. These basic pieces are the ones you should sew together when you're making a muslin. It helps you understand the construction of the garment, test the fit, and approve of the style. Remember, keep the pieces of your project in mind when you're looking for a vintage linen to use, and know that you can incorporate small textiles for something like a collar, a sleeve, or a cuff. Even though many of the home décor projects in the book aren't made from purchased patterns, the same principle of thinking in pieces applies to those items as well.

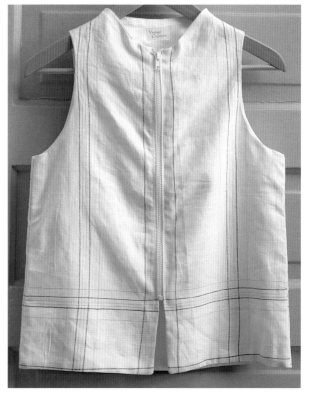

This top was made from a very simple but stylish pattern.

FINISHING TECHNIQUES

As in normal garment sewing, you must finish the outer edges with a facing, a lining, or a hem. You can also finish edges by lining all or part of the garment. A lining piece is usually cut from the same pattern piece as the part it will line. Vests and yokes are usually lined as a simple way to finish off the outer edges. Linings can be very helpful in sewing with vintage fabrics—to back a sheer fabric, for example. Look at the Dress with Crocheted Yoke on page 78 to see how the lined yoke allows you to use a delicate fabric with an airy, open weave.

Children's clothes are often finished off with binding that you make yourself. Curved edges need a binding cut on the bias—the diagonal direction of the fabric—which offers stretch and give. This gives the binding flexibility around the curves. Children's clothes also often use plackets for their back openings, and I've substituted them for other finishing techniques in some of the projects in this book. See the sidebar below for instructions on making a placket.

Edge-to-Edge Stitching. This is a specialized technique of sewing laces, trims, or other delicate textiles to one another or to a finished edge. You must use extrafine thread while stitching edge-to-edge, and note that it needs to be threaded through the machine and the bobbin. (You may see this thread referred to as lingerie-weight thread.) Furthermore, you need to

Making a Placket

Construct a placket by making a slash down the middle of the garment (front or back, wherever you're placing the placket). Your placket strip needs to be twice the length of your slash. I usually make my placket strips about 1½ to 2 inches wide and trim off the excess. After you've cut the strip, pull the slash so the opening is practically straight and apply the placket strip. After stitching, trim the seam. Finish the raw edge of the placket strip or fold under the raw edge of the placket. Press the placket strip to the inside of the garment, covering the seam. Stitch along the folded edge. On the inside, stitch through all thicknesses at a slant.

  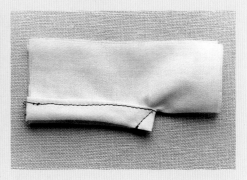

use a sharp, fine needle when you use extrafine thread. For this technique, place the two edges you're joining right side up with the edges abutting one another (not overlapping). Use a medium zigzag stitch to join the pieces together, as shown at the right.

Vintage Sewing Considerations

Here are a few things to keep in mind when you're working with these irreplaceable textiles.

Here is an example of edge-to-edge stitching, shown with dark thread for ease of viewing. In actual practice, you should use a color of thread that matches your lace.

USE THE RIGHT THREAD AND NEEDLE

For many of these projects, regular sewing thread is fine. But for some, extrafine or lingerie-weight thread is the best choice, because it's designed for delicate textiles like lace. It's also inconspicuous. Anytime you use edge-to-edge stitching, you should be using extrafine thread. Again—be sure you have the thread in the bobbin of your machine, and don't forget that sharp, fine needle, size 9 (70).

Invisible thread is sometimes recommended when you don't want your stitches to be seen at all. The project instructions will tell you if any of these specialty threads are required.

NOTCH OR CLIP THE CURVES

For proper fit and give, curves should either be clipped or notched: inner curves should be clipped, and outer curves should be notched.

FINISH THE SEAMS

There's a saying that the inside of your garment should be as pretty as the outside. I don't follow that exactly, but your inside seams should be finished to keep them from raveling, particularly with a special vintage fabric. You can finish a seam by using a simple zigzag stitch, which is quick and easy. French seams, shown at the right, are the industry standard on fine children's garments. To make a French seam: Place the *wrong* sides of the fabric together and stitch using a ¼-inch seam allowance. Trim the seam to ⅛ inch. Turn and press. Now, with *right* sides together, stitch using a ¼-inch seam allowance, encasing the other seam.

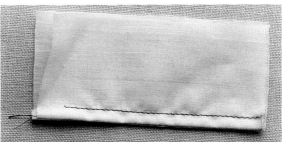

French seams are a stylish way to finish a seam. In the photos above, at top, the fabric pieces are joined with the wrong sides facing. In the bottom photo, the seam has been trimmed and the fabric turned with the right sides together as the final seam is stitched.

How is Lace Made?

Centuries ago, lace was all made by hand, using either the bobbin or needle techniques. Bobbin lace was woven around pins, plaited, or otherwise manipulated using many threads simultaneously. Needle lace, on the other hand, was made with needle and thread, built up by the stitch. Machines can now imitate both techniques.

If you have a serger (a fabulous machine that also trims seams as it stitches), you can serge the seams to finish. Sergers are great, but they can't replace your regular sewing machine.

MAKING ADJUSTMENTS TO PIECES FROM A PURCHASED PATTERN

Sometimes the size of your vintage linen may cause you to make some adjustments to an individual pattern piece—a good example is the Reversible Wrap Skirt on page 125. I had to cut one piece into two so I could place them to take best advantage of the design on my tablecloth. Take a look at that project to see how you can quickly alter a pattern piece if necessary. It's also easy to create your own facing if you need to, as I did in the Scalloped Edge Jacket on page 87. If you find a complicated pattern you really like, perhaps you can simplify it. For example, I almost never make welted pockets because they're so labor intensive. I might apply a simple patch pocket instead, or just omit it altogether.

ADDING DECORATIVE ELEMENTS

Part of the beauty of sewing with vintage textiles is how much character they add to a garment or home accessory, and sometimes you only need to add a decorative border or edging to achieve a beautiful look. In the Curtains with Checked Borders project on page 118, I added a decorative border at the hem, and I used a similar technique on the Handkerchief Yoke Dress on page 40. I added a wide piece of lace to the upper back of the Lattice Blouse on page 58. The project section is full of ways to use vintage linens as embellishments and is loaded with helpful tips.

If you follow the basic rules of sewing for clothing or home accessories, you should have no trouble working with vintage textiles. Use the quick guide on page 27 if you need help with a specific topic, so you can see how I addressed a particular issue while I was making a project. Remember that you have options when you're constructing a piece—add a facing, leave one out, alter a hemline. That's part of the creativity of sewing that I love, and hope you will, too.

Using the Project Instructions

Now you're getting to the fun part: choosing a project to make. Here's what you'll find in the pages that follow: 32 garment and home décor projects using a wide range of vintage textiles. All of the garments were made from purchased patterns, as were a few of the home accessories, and you'll find the pattern names and numbers with each project. As you'll need to purchase the patterns to make these projects, I haven't included the complete sewing instructions. But I have given you directions for any alterations that I made to incorporate the vintage fabrics. The remaining projects are custom designs that you'll construct from patterns made from tracing paper or make from pieces that you'll simply cut directly from the fabric.

While I've given you a general list of the notions you need, consult the envelopes of the purchased patterns for specific information. Although the yardage requirements give you a basic idea of whether you have enough fabric to construct your home accessory or garment, actually laying out the pattern pieces is still the best course of action. For the projects that aren't made from purchased patterns, you'll find the notions you need listed in the instructions.

Each project has a layout sketch to help you re-create the look I achieved. You can see how I approached each type of textile in relation to the individual pieces of that project. Remember, too, that you won't be using the same vintage fabrics I found, but you can take the ideas presented and adapt them to your own projects. If you have a small rectangular piece that's begging to be used, see the bolster pillow on

front   front facing   front

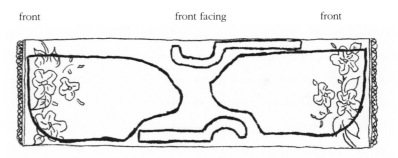

Fig. 1   front facing

sleeve front

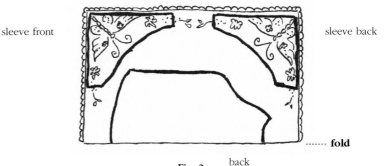

sleeve back

Fig. 2   back   **fold**

The layout sketches will help you understand how I incorporated the design elements of the vintage fabrics used in this book. The blouse pictured at the left in the top photo is made of two different linens, as shown in these sketches.

page 50. Find a great tablecloth with appliqué? See the appliquéd pieces used in the dress on page 100 and the purse on page 98. Variations of many of the projects are included, so you can see how using different linens or trim can create a completely new look.

Sewing with vintage fabrics allows you to be resourceful and imaginative while preserving a bit of the past. While sewing used to be an inexpensive way to make clothes and home accessories, it has transcended that functional level to become fine art. When you incorporate a vintage textile, you're creating a unique piece with charm and grace that expresses your creativity. You can also combine your other artistic skills with a vintage garment; if you have some of your grandmother's yarn and can knit, make a collar for a vest. Or maybe you can combine ribbon embroidery into a pillow made from antique linen. Use all of your skills when you sew with these distinctive vintage fabrics.

Not Enough Fabric?

This is one of the most common problems you'll encounter when sewing with vintage textiles. To solve it, piece the fabric pieces together, so to speak. For instance, I once used a white linen with a lovely striped border to make a blouse, and wanted to have the stripes on the sleeves, too. But I didn't have enough fabric left to cut out the entire sleeve. Instead, I cut the sleeve out of a matching white linen and applied the leftover striped fabric to the hem of the sleeve.

It worked beautifully and was very attractive, too; in fact, take a look at it on page 122.

Remember that you can always mix fabrics, which will add a great deal of charm to your project. Add a hem, or a cuff, or a collar from a contrasting fabric, or make a stool slipcover with the top from one fabric and the skirt from another. Not only are you solving a problem, you're making a great design choice, too!

Quick Guide to Tips and Alterations

In addition to the information presented in the preceding section, here's an index to the tips and alterations you'll find in the project section of *Sewing with Fabulous Vintage Fabrics.*

Basic Sewing Supplies

Here's a list of the materials and supplies that you need to have on hand for every project. If you need a special material, or the project calls for a specialized use for that item, the instructions will list it.

Lightweight tracing paper

Water-soluble marking pens

Paper scissors

Sewing shears and scissors

Seam ripper

Silk pins

Magnetic pin holder

Tape measure

Sewing gauge

White and ecru extrafine thread

Invisible thread

Sewing machine

Sharp machine needles (medium and fine)

Sharp hand needles

Thimble

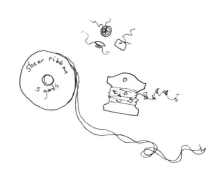

Luxurious Fabrics...
Linens, Lace & More

Linen Napkin Pillow

Vintage linen, an antique mother-of-pearl button, and sumptuous velveteen combine to make a beautiful pillow.

You Will Need

- BASIC SEWING SUPPLIES
- EXTRAFINE THREAD
- LARGE LINEN NAPKIN, WITH EMBROIDERY AND TRIM (ABOUT 16 X 16 INCHES)
- ½ YARD OF VELVETEEN
- 1 MOTHER-OF-PEARL BUTTON
- PILLOW FORM (14 X 14 INCHES)

Layout and Construction

1 For the Front, cut 1 piece of velveteen that is 15 x 15 inches. For the Back, cut 2 pieces of velveteen that are each 15 x 17 inches.

2 Open the linen napkin and lay it flat. Cut the napkin into four equal parts (figure 1).

3 Place the napkin pieces on top of the velveteen Front, with the lace edges meeting in the middle. Pin all the edges down. Zigzag around all the edges of the napkin, stitching it to the velveteen Front (figure 2). Sew the button into the middle of the Front, where the edges of the napkin meet.

4 Take the 15 x 17-inch pieces of velveteen and fold them in half so they are 15 x 8½ inches. With right sides together, place one of the Back pieces on the left side of the Front, raw edges meeting, and the fold in the middle. Now, place the other piece on the right side of the Front, also matching raw edges (figure 3). They will overlap in the middle, and this will serve as the opening to insert your pillow form. Stitch around the pillow in a ½-inch seam. Trim the seam, turn, and press. Insert the pillow form.

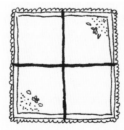

Fig. 1

Fig. 2

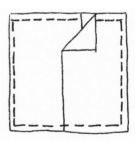

Fig. 3

Embellished Blouses

The dainty butterflies that adorn the sleeves of the blouse on the left once decorated a bridge cloth. The variation on the right features sleeves accented with drawnwork.

Layout and Construction

1 Lay the table runner flat so the embroidery is at the ends. Place the Front and Front Facing pattern pieces on the table runner; the embroidery should fall at the bottom of the Front pieces as shown (figure 1). Cut out each piece separately.

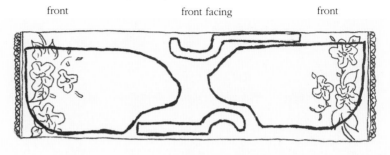

Fig. 1

2 Fold the bridge cloth and cut the Sleeve Front, Sleeve Back, and Back. Study the construction of this raglan sleeve; if you have an embroidered item like a butterfly, make sure its orientation is correct before you cut. Since this piece had butterflies embroidered on all four corners, both Sleeve pieces (Front and Back) were cut on these corners. The Back was cut on the fold from the undecorated portion of the linen (figure 2).

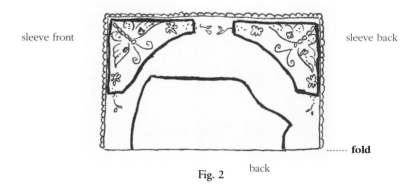

Fig. 2

3 Follow the instructions in the pattern envelope for construction. Add shoulder pads and lace edging to the sleeves, if desired.

Tip: The Butterfly Blouse demonstrates how you can easily use small linens in an adult garment by taking advantage of the blouse's design. The two-piece raglan sleeve presents a great opportunity to incorporate a napkin, a handkerchief, or a special piece of embroidery like these butterflies.

Variation: White Embroidered Blouse with Drawnwork

You Will Need

- BASIC SEWING SUPPLIES

- ROUND WHITE EMBROIDERED TABLECLOTH WITH LACE

- WHITE TABLECLOTH WITH DRAWNWORK

- 100 PERCENT COTTON SHEET OR LINING FABRIC

- 4 LARGE SNAPS

- SHOULDER PADS (OPTIONAL)

Pattern

CUTTING LINE DESIGNS: BY POPULAR DEMAND #60565

Pattern Pieces

- FRONT

- BACK

- SLEEVE FRONT

- SLEEVE BACK

- FRONT FACING

Layout and Construction

1 Cut the Front from the folded round linen tablecloth (figure 3); if your tablecloth has lace, save it to apply to the sleeves.

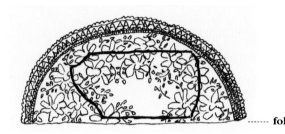

Fig. 3   front

2 Cut the Back, Sleeve Front, and Sleeve Back from the tablecloth with drawnwork (figure 4). Place the Back so the bottom displays the drawnwork. In this project, the drawnwork on the sleeves cascades down the shoulders from the neckline.

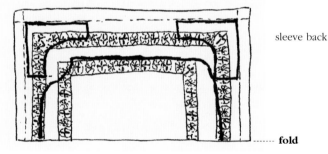

sleeve front   sleeve back

Fig. 4   back

3 Place the Front Facing on the folded cotton sheet or lining material and cut out the pieces.

4 Follow the instructions in the pattern envelope for construction, adding to the sleeves the lace that you saved in step 1. I substituted snaps for buttons in this variation.

Pattern Courtesy of Cutting Line Designs: By Popular Demand #60565

Quilted Collage Collection

Don't let your beautiful scraps go to waste! Instead, use this technique for making fabric collages on quilt batting.

Quilted Collage Collection

You Will Need

- BASIC SEWING SUPPLIES
- SCRAPS OF LINEN AND LACE
- QUILT BATTING
- LINING FABRIC
- EXTRAFINE THREAD
- BUTTONS, SNAPS, OR HOOK-AND-LOOP TAPE
- BUTTONS, BEADS, AND/OR RIBBONS
- SPECIALTY THREADS OR FIBERS

Making the Collage

Because I use a lot of fabric collage in many different projects, I make a square yard at a time. But you can use this technique to make a smaller square, of course—just make sure that your layers are all the same size. A square yard will be enough to make a small, medium, and large bag, with left-over fabric for the bookmarks.

Create a fabric collage by laying remnants of linen and lace on top of the lining fabric. To begin, cut the lining fabric into two squares, each 36 x 36 inches. Cut one piece of batting that is also 36 x 36 inches. Layer the pieces as following: lining, batting, and lining. Pin these layers together and stitch around the outside edges with a long running stitch.

Don't let the actual design of the collage make you nervous! If you take your time, you can create a beautiful design. To get the most visual impact from linens that have decorative corners, cut them diagonally. I sometimes cut up small cocktail napkins or use the edges of old handkerchiefs. Any linen remnant that has pretty work on it is a good choice for this project. Place different colors beside each other for contrast, or vary white and off-white if you don't want a lot of color. Add the pieces of lace last. Incorporate them for contrast and to cover any visible raw edges. When you're happy with your design, pin it in place using *lots* of pins (figure 1). Pin down all the edges. Baste all the pieces down by hand, being sure to go through all the layers.

Stitch your collage on the machine using a zigzag stitch. As you stitch through all the layers, you're quilting the top. This stitching will take a while, as you'll have lots of edges to sew. When you finish your piece, clip all the threads on top and underneath.

Fig. 1

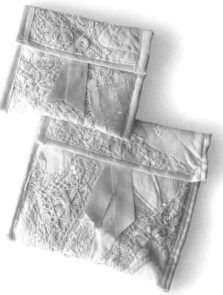

Layout and Construction (Bags)

1 Make simple bags to the size you prefer, using this easy method. Decide how large you want your bag. Figure the length, double that amount, and add 2 or more inches to allow for the flap. Cut the fabric to this length by the desired width of your bag. Zigzag the raw edges after you've cut your piece. Now, simply fold the bottom up to your desired depth and zigzag the sides together. Here are some general measurements to use:

To make a **small** bag, cut a piece of fabric collage that is 5 inches wide x 12 inches long. Fold the bottom up 5 inches, pin, and stitch. You now have a bag that is 5 inches wide x 7 inches high. Fold a 2-inch flap over to the front.

To make a **medium** bag, cut a piece of fabric collage that is 10 inches wide x 23 inches long. Fold the bottom up 10 inches, pin, and stitch. You now have a bag that is 10 inches wide x 13 inches high. Fold a 3-inch flap over to the front.

To make a **large** bag, cut a piece of fabric collage that is 15 inches wide x 35 inches long. Fold the bottom up 15 inches, pin, and stitch. You now have a bag that is 15 inches wide x 20 inches high. Fold a 5-inch flap over to the front.

2 You can leave the side edges as they are or encase them with ribbon or binding. Pin a piece of ribbon to the edge, with half of the ribbon extended over the edge and the ends of the ribbon folded under. Stitch the ribbon to the fabric at the edge of the ribbon using small stitches. Fold the ribbon over and stitch it the same way on the other side.

3 For closures, you can make a buttonhole in the top flap and sew on a pretty button; use snaps; or add hook-and-loop tape. For additional decoration, cross two pieces of ribbon and sew them to the underside of the flap (figure 2).

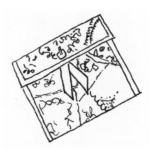

Fig. 2

Layout and Construction (Bookmarks)

1 Take some of the fabric collage and cut it into bookmark shapes. Vary the sizes, if you'd like. Finish the edges as in step 2 at the left. Use specialty threads or fibers to hang over the end of the bookmark, serving as the "marker" outside the book. Take strands of three different specialty threads and twist them together, zigzag them to the bookmark, and then tie the threads in a knot at the top of the bookmark. Add beads or buttons to the various threads, knotting between each bead or button (figure 3).

Tip: Don't be intimidated by designing and making these collaged items. It's fun, and it's a great opportunity to incorporate all sorts of lovely laces, great buttons, beautiful beads, etc., into your sewing. Look for these specialty threads and fibers at fabric shops and at craft stores— they're used often in scrapbooking.

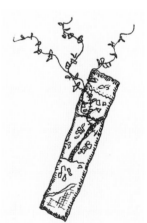

Fig. 3

Lavender Floral Dress

As lovely as a spring day, this dress demonstrates how one beautiful textile can be transformed into a darling garment; its variations blossom with linens and lace.

You Will Need
- BASIC SEWING SUPPLIES
- TABLECLOTH WITH FLORAL MOTIFS
- EXTRAFINE THREAD
- 1 VINTAGE BUTTON
- RIBBON, IN A MATCHING COLOR
- SAFETY PIN

Pattern
THE CHILDREN'S CORNER PATTERNS: HILLARY

Pattern Pieces
- SKIRT FRONT
- SKIRT BACK
- YOKE FRONT
- YOKE BACK
- SLEEVE B

Note:
USE EXTRAFINE THREAD AND ¼-INCH SEAM ALLOWANCES THROUGHOUT, UNLESS DIRECTED OTHERWISE.

Pattern Alteration
Make this change while following the instructions in the pattern envelope:

Back Closure
Omit the tie in the back of each of these dresses and use a button closure instead.

Layout and Construction

1 Fold the tablecloth. Place the Skirt Front and the Skirt Back so large bouquets of flowers are centered across them. If your tablecloth has a colorful overcast edging like this one, or has any other decorative treatment you want to highlight, use it as the hem of the dress, but remember to add some extra length to allow for the growth of your child. Place the Yoke Front, Yoke Back, and Sleeve so smaller bouquets of flowers are centered on these pieces (figure 1). Cut the facings and linings now, too.

2 Follow the pattern's instructions for construction, noting the back closure change listed above. I also added a decorative bow.

Tip: Bows should always be pinned onto the dress from the inside, so they can be removed for washing or replaced later with fresh ribbon.

yoke front   yoke front lining

back

fold

front

yoke back

yoke back lining

sleeve

sleeve lining

Fig. 1

Variation: Handkerchief Yoke Dress

You Will Need
- BASIC SEWING SUPPLIES
- HANDKERCHIEF(S)
- IMITATION BATISTE
- LACE DOILY
- EXTRAFINE THREAD
- BRIDGE CLOTH WITH CUTWORK AND DECORATIVE EDGING
- TATTING
- 1 VINTAGE BUTTON

Pattern
THE CHILDREN'S CORNER PATTERNS: HILLARY

Pattern Pieces
- SKIRT FRONT
- SKIRT BACK
- YOKE FRONT
- YOKE BACK
- SLEEVE B

Note:
USE EXTRAFINE THREAD AND ¼-INCH SEAM ALLOWANCES THROUGHOUT, UNLESS DIRECTED OTHERWISE.

Pattern Alteration
Note the change listed on page 38 of this book while following the pattern's instructions.

Layout and Construction

1 Because this dress is a small size, I was able to cut the Yoke Front and Yoke Back out of one vintage handkerchief. (I chose a sheer white handkerchief with cutwork.) Fold the handkerchief and place the yoke pattern pieces, being sure to put the Yoke Front on the fold (figure 2). Cut these pieces; they'll be lined.

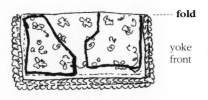

yoke back — yoke front — fold

Fig. 2

2 Fold the lace doily and cut the Sleeve (figure 3). Fold the imitation batiste and cut the Skirt Front, Skirt Back, and lining pieces.

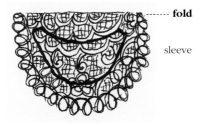

fold — sleeve

Fig. 3

3 Follow the pattern's instructions for construction, noting the back closure alteration listed on page 38.

4 To add the decorative hem edging, first cut off 7 inches from opposite ends of the bridge cloth (figure 4). Each piece should be 7 x 36 inches (figure 5). Since the skirt is just a little wider than 72 inches, I solved this problem by making an adjustment in the skirt: I took up the side seams until the skirt was 72 inches around the bottom.

Fig. 4

Fig. 5

5 Finish the raw edge of each piece of the bridge cloth. Make a 1-inch machine hem on the dress, and mark a seamline all the way around the dress that is 6 inches from the bottom. Pin the bridge cloth edging to the dress, wrong side of the edging to the right side of the Skirt Front at the marked seamline. Pin the other piece of bridge cloth edging to the Skirt Back. Zigzag along the seamline. Stitch the edging down at the side seams. (Alternately, you can also add a decorative hem by stitching the pieces together, right sides facing, as in the hem for the Curtains with Checked Borders, step 4, page 119.)

6 Hand sew the tatting along the bottom edges of the Yoke Front and Yoke Back.

Tip: Remember that this is a very small dress size, so I was able to cut both of the yoke pieces from one handkerchief. If you're making a larger size, you may need to use more than one handkerchief.

Variation: *Dress with Lace Handkerchief Sleeves*

You Will Need

Pattern

THE CHILDREN'S CORNER PATTERNS: HILLARY

Pattern Pieces

- SKIRT FRONT
- SKIRT BACK
- YOKE FRONT
- YOKE BACK
- SLEEVE B

Note:

USE EXTRAFINE THREAD AND ¼-INCH SEAM ALLOWANCES THROUGHOUT, UNLESS DIRECTED OTHERWISE.

Pattern Alteration

Note the change listed on page 38 of this book while following the pattern's instructions.

Layout and Construction

1 This variation features sleeves with appliquéd handkerchiefs and a beautiful medallion of Irish lace appliquéd onto the Yoke Front. Cut the Skirt Front, Skirt Back, and Sleeve from the folded tablecloth. Cut the Yoke Front and Yoke Back as in step 1 of the Handkerchief Yoke Dress. Cut the linings from the lining fabric.

2 To make the handkerchief appliqué for the Sleeve, fold the handkerchief diagonally. Place the Sleeve pattern over the hand-kerchief (figure 6). With a water-soluble marker, trace around the edge of the pattern. Cut this piece out. Pin the handkerchief piece onto the Sleeve, wrong side of the handkerchief piece to the right side of the Sleeve (figure 7), and stitch to each Sleeve using a tight zigzag stitch. Line the Sleeve as directed in the pattern instructions.

3 Follow the pattern's instructions for construction, noting the back closure alteration listed on page 38.

4 Hand sew the tatting along the bottom edges of the Yoke Front and Yoke Back. Hand sew the Irish lace medallion to the middle of the Yoke Front.

Pattern Courtesy of The Children's Corner Patterns: Hillary

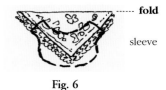

Fig. 6

Fig. 7

Ruffled Chair Skirt

These graceful skirts sew up so easily that you can create a whole wardrobe of them for your chairs, changing the skirts as your heart desires.

You Will Need

- BASIC SEWING SUPPLIES
- LIGHTWEIGHT TRACING PAPER
- LARGE PATTERNED TABLECLOTH
- NARROW RIBBON

Layout and Construction

1 First, precisely measure the top of your chair seat. The trickiest part will be getting the back corners right, where the legs meet the seat (figure 1). Put a piece of tracing paper on the chair and trace the seat, then add the ½-inch seam allowance around the circumference. Use this custom pattern piece for the Seat.

2 Now, so you can cut the Skirt, measure the circumference of your chair and double this figure. (If necessary, you can sew strips together to reach the proper length.) This Skirt is 4 inches long, and I added ½ inch to each side for the seam allowance and the hem. Cut the ruffle to these measurements: 5 inches by the doubled circumference of your chair. (In this project, my chair measured 62 inches in circumference, so I needed 5-inch-wide strips that would equal 124 inches in length.) Lay the tablecloth flat and cut all of the pieces out (figure 2).

3 Stitch the Skirt pieces together (figure 3). Finish one of the raw edges with a zigzag stitch or a serger. Make a ½-inch machine hem.

4 Machine hem the two corners of the Seat in the back; you'll add the ribbon ties here later (figure 4). As there needs to be a break in your Skirt between the back legs of the chair, you'll add a separate piece of the ruffle here. Measure the length of this area and double it. Cut off a piece of the ruffle to this measurement and use it for the back section of the Skirt. Gather the top edge of both pieces of the ruffle.

5 Stitch the longer portion of the ruffled Skirt to the front and sides of the Seat using a ½-inch seam allowance, right sides together. Stitch the shorter portion of the Skirt to the Seat between the two back corners, right sides together. Sew ribbon ties to the wrong side of the Skirt at the back and front corners (figure 5).

Fig. 1

ruffle strips

seat   **Fig. 2**

Fig. 3

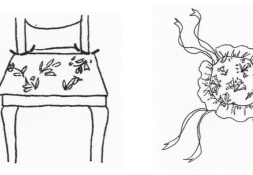

Fig. 4   **Fig. 5**

Variation: Matelasse Chair Skirt

You Will Need

- BASIC SEWING SUPPLIES
- LIGHTWEIGHT TRACING PAPER
- MATELASSE BEDSPREAD WITH SCALLOPED HEM
- NARROW RIBBON

Layout and Construction

1 Follow the instructions for making the custom pattern piece for the Seat as in the Ruffled Chair Skirt (step 1 on page 45). Because the Skirt in this variation is not gathered, use the directions below to add the Skirt.

2 Measure the circumference of your chair and add 4 inches. The Skirt length in this variation is 4½ inches, plus ½ inch added for the seam allowance. Cut the Skirt to these measurements. (For example, the circumference of my chair is 62 inches, so I cut a Skirt that was 5 x 66 inches). Cut the Seat and Skirt from the unfolded bedspread, placing the Skirt along the scalloped edge (figure 6).

3 Finish the back corners as in the Ruffled Chair Skirt (step 4 on page 45). Measure the distance between the legs in the back as in step 4 on page 45 to determine the break in the back of the Skirt. (This is where you'll tie the seat cover to the legs.) Cut off this much of the scalloped edging, plus 1 inch. Turn under ½ inch at the ends of both skirt pieces and stitch.

4 With right sides together, stitch the longer portion of the Skirt to the front and sides of the Seat in a ½ inch seam, gathering at the corners as necessary. Stitch the shorter portion of the Skirt to the Seat between the two back corners. Apply ribbons to the back and front corners as in step 5 of the Ruffled Chair Skirt (figure 5 on page 45).

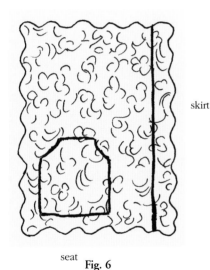

skirt

seat **Fig. 6**

Variation: Linen and Lace Skirt

Layout and Construction

1 Follow the instructions for making the custom pattern piece for the Seat as in the Ruffled Chair Skirt (step 1 on page 45). Place this piece on the unfolded linen and cut it out (figure 7). Finish the back corners as in the Ruffled Chair Skirt (step 4 on page 45).

2 To add the lace Skirt, measure the circumference of your chair and add 4 inches. (In this variation, the chair is 62 inches so I needed 66 inches of lace.) Measure the distance between the legs in the back as you did in step 4 on page 45 to determine the break in the back of the Skirt. (This is where you'll tie the seat cover to the legs.) Cut off this much of the lace, plus 1 inch. Turn under ½ inch at the ends of both lace pieces and stitch.

You Will Need

- LIGHTWEIGHT TRACING PAPER
- SHEER LINEN
- EXTRAFINE THREAD
- LACE, AT LEAST 3 INCHES WIDE AND A LITTLE LONGER THE CIRCUMFERENCE OF YOUR CHAIR
- NARROW RIBBON

Fig. 7   seat

3 Apply the lace Skirt to the Seat by placing it on the ½-inch seamline, wrong side of the lace to the right side of the Seat, and zigzag the lace to the Seat in a narrow stitch. Stitch the longer portion of the lace Skirt to the front and sides of the Seat, gathering at the corners as necessary. Stitch the shorter portion of the lace Skirt to the Seat between the two back corners. Apply ribbons to the back and front corners as in step 5 of the Ruffled Chair Skirt (figure 5 on page 45).

Elegant Eyeglass Case

Safeguard your spectacles in a simple little bag embellished with vintage braid and a unique old button.

You Will Need

- BASIC SEWING SUPPLIES

- SMALL TEXTILE OR PURCHASED FABRIC

- EXTRAFINE THREAD

- VINTAGE TRIM

- 1 VINTAGE BUTTON

Fig. 1

Fig. 2

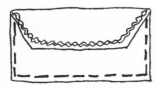

Fig. 3

Fig. 4

Layout and Construction

1 Cut a piece for the case that is 10 inches wide x 8¼ inches high. Cut a piece for the flap that is 9 inches wide x 2¼ inches high.

2 To create the angled flap, fold under ½ inch on one raw edge and press. Then, fold in the outer edges of the flap and pin. Stitch the edges in place using extrafine thread (figure 1). Center the flap onto the case, right sides together, leaving ½ inch on either side of the flap (figure 2). Stitch using a narrow ¼-inch seam allowance. Press the flap open.

3 Add the trim along the edge of the flap, wrong side of the trim to the right side of the flap, using thread that matches the color of the trim. Press the flap down to the front and edgestitch along the top of the flap, encasing the narrow seam. Finish the remaining raw edges by serging or zigzag stitch. Make narrow ½-inch machine hems along each side of the case (figure 3).

4 Fold the case in half, placing the bottom under the flap. Stitch the sides together, wrong sides facing (figure 4). Add a button-hole and the vintage button to finish.

Tip: This little case would also make a lovely envelope for a special greeting.

Alternative: See the Quilted Collage Collection on page 35 to learn a different method of constructing a bag.

Peach Bolster Pillow

Coordinate two different linens to create this classy bolster; it's the perfect use for a small rectangular piece, like this quilted dresser accessory.

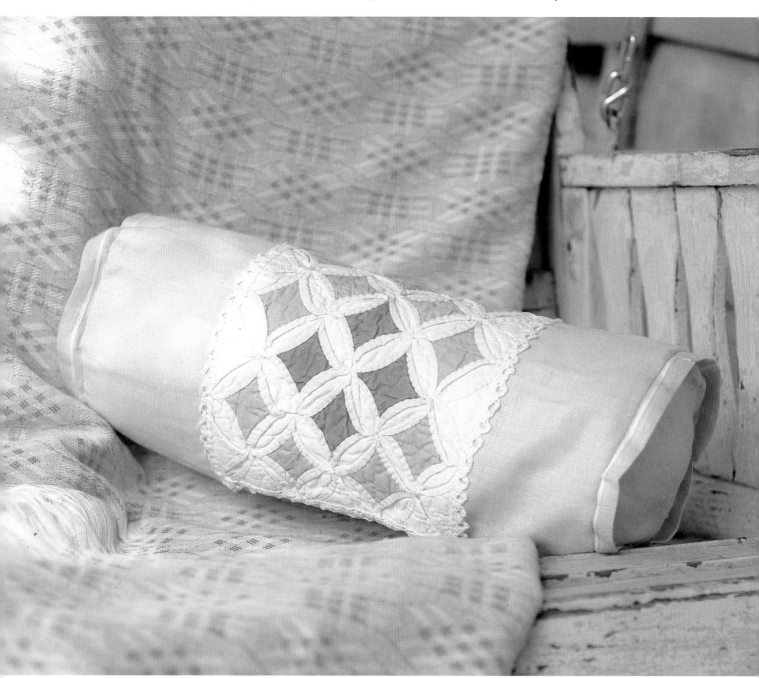

You Will Need

BASIC SEWING SUPPLIES

QUILTED PIECE (AS LONG AS THE CIRCUMFERENCE OF YOUR PILLOW FORM, PLUS AT LEAST 3 INCHES)

4 TO 6 NAPKINS OR OTHER SMALL LINENS

4 SNAPS

BOLSTER PILLOW FORM (19 X 15 INCHES)

Layout and Construction

1 Cut one of the napkins in half (figure 1). Place one of the halves on top of the other; if your napkins have edging, the edging on the top half should lie directly on top of the edging on the half underneath (figure 2). Stitch them together along the edging.

2 Repeat step 1 with a second napkin, to create two long pieces. Place the quilted piece between the napkin pieces, wrong side of the quilted piece to the right side of the napkins, overlapping about ¾ inch (figure 3). Stitch the quilted piece to the napkins along each edge.

3 If your quilted piece is longer than the napkins, trim the excess to make it the same length as the napkins and zigzag or serge to finish the edge. Wrap the piece around the pillow form, overlapping the edges, with the quilted piece's original edge on top. Pin the cover closed; mark where the fabrics meet to establish the stitching line. Remove the pillow.

4 Leaving the piece overlapped and pinned, stitch each end for about 2 inches; leave the middle free to create an opening to insert the pillow (figure 4). Sew snaps along the opening.

5 Measure the diameter of the pillow form. Cut the round ends to these measurements, using one napkin for each end (figure 5); remember to include a seam allowance. Save the edging.

Fig. 1

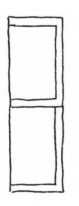

Fig. 2

Fig. 3

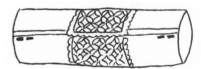

Fig. 4

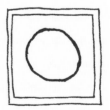

Fig. 5

Peach Bolster Pillow

6 If desired, take the leftover edging from the pieces you used in step 5 and trim them to 1 inch wide. Sew these pieces of edging together (figure 6) and make two long strips to use as piping around the ends of the bolster.

7 Insert the pillow form and pin around the edges where you'll place the edging, marking the end of the pillow with a water-soluble marker. Remove the pillow form. Pin the edging to the pillow, right sides together, and stitch on the marked seamline (figure 7).

8 Trim the seam to ¼ inch. Turn the pillow inside out and pin the ends to the pillow (figure 8). Stitch using a ¼-inch seam allowance.

9 Turn the pillow, press, and insert the form. Snap the opening closed.

Note: I purchased this unusual little quilted thing at an estate sale, and it's one of the more intriguing items I've found. It was created to display brooches on a dresser by pinning them into the quilted top.

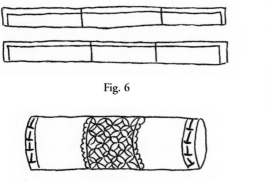

Fig. 6

Fig. 7

Fig. 8

Curtain Panel Blouse

This elegant blouse is cleverly constructed from sheer curtain panels. The versatility of this pattern allows you to achieve many different looks.

Curtain Panel Blouse

You Will Need

- BASIC SEWING SUPPLIES
- SHEER EMBROIDERED CURTAIN PANELS
- LINEN SHEET OR OTHER LIGHTWEIGHT, BUT NOT SHEER, FABRIC
- 11 VINTAGE BUTTONS

Pattern

- THE SEWING WORKSHOP: CHOPIN BLOUSE

Pattern Pieces

- FRONT
- FRONT POCKET OVERLAY
- UPPER BACK
- NECK BAND
- UNDER CUFF
- GODET
- LOWER BACK
- UNDER COLLAR
- SLEEVE PLACKET
- SLEEVE

Pattern Alterations

Make these changes while following the instructions in the pattern envelope:

Collar and Cuff

Since you're using linens that provide a unique look, omit the instructions for shirring the collar and cuffs. Because you're not shirring these pieces, you won't need the Upper Collar, Upper Cuff, and Strap, and will use the Under pattern pieces instead.

Front

Although the pattern's instructions direct you to hem the front early in the construction of the blouse, wait to hem it until the garment is finished.

Front Pocket Overlay

Use the Front Pocket Overlay, but don't complete the stitching that creates the pocket. Stitch down the sides of the Overlay, but you can let the bottom hang freely if desired.

Back

Sew the Lower Back to the Upper Back lining rather than to the Upper Back, allowing the Upper Back to hang freely and display the edging of the linen. If your linen doesn't have an edging, you can add tatting, lace, or fringe to the lower edge of the Upper Back.

Layout and Construction

1 Fold the fabric. Since these curtain panels had such pretty edges, I cut some of the pieces to incorporate the edges. For this look, place the bottom of the Godet, the front edge of the Front Pocket Overlay, the bottom of the Upper Back, and the bottom edge of the Under Cuff on the scalloped edges of the linen. Arrange the other pieces as indicated (figure 1). Note that you need to cut four Sleeve Plackets.

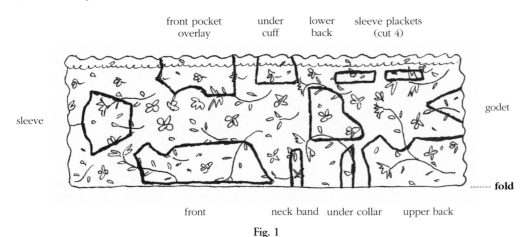

Fig. 1

2 Cut the linings for the Upper Back, Under Collar, Under Cuff, Sleeve Placket, and Neck Band out of the lightweight fabric (figure 2). Again, note that you need to cut four Sleeve Placket lining pieces.

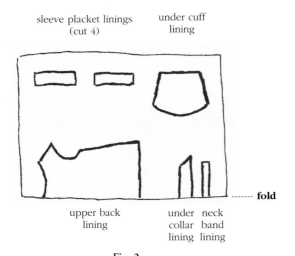

Fig. 2

3 Follow the pattern's instructions for construction, noting the alterations listed on page 54.

Tip: Sheer linens can be limiting unless you have a pattern that incorporates layers. I love this pattern because the layers allow you to "line" the pieces that need it and use beautiful sheer linens on the sleeves, lower front, and lower back, as in this project.

Variation: Strawberry Tablecloth Blouse

You Will Need

BASIC SEWING SUPPLIES

100 PERCENT LINEN OR COTTON SHEET

SMALL COLORFUL TABLECLOTH, WITH A BACKGROUND COLOR THAT MATCHES THE SHEETING

12 VINTAGE BUTTONS

FRINGE (OPTIONAL)

Pattern

THE SEWING WORKSHOP: CHOPIN BLOUSE

Pattern Pieces

FRONT

FRONT POCKET OVERLAY

UPPER BACK

NECK BAND

UNDER CUFF

GODET

LOWER BACK

UNDER COLLAR

SLEEVE PLACKET

SLEEVE

Pattern Alterations

Note the changes listed on page 54 of this book while following the pattern's instructions.

Layout and Construction

1 Fold the tablecloth. Cut the Front Pocket Overlay, Under Cuff, Godet, and Under Collar (figure 3). If your tablecloth has fringe, save it to apply to the bottom of the Lower Back and the Godet, if desired.

under cuff

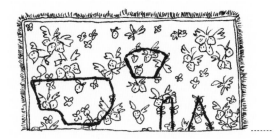

fold

front pocket overlay   under collar godet

Fig. 3

2 Fold the linen or cotton sheet and cut the following:

Front (two), Upper Back (two on fold—one is for lining), Lower Back (two), Sleeve, (two), Under Cuff (two for lining), Collar (one on fold for lining), Neck Band (two on fold—one is for lining), and Sleeve Plackets (eight—four are for lining).

3 Follow the pattern's instructions for construction, noting the alterations listed on page 54. Add the fringe as desired to the lower back.

Tip: Here's another example of successfully using a linen that has a small amount of yardage—cut just a few pieces from it, like the overlay, cuffs, and collar in this pattern. Then, pair those pieces with a coordinating linen.

Variation: Lattice Blouse

You Will Need

- BASIC SEWING SUPPLIES
- 100 PERCENT COTTON SHEET
- LATTICEWORK OR OTHER EMBELLISHED LINEN
- 12 VINTAGE BUTTONS
- LACE (OPTIONAL)

Pattern

- THE SEWING WORKSHOP: CHOPIN BLOUSE

Pattern Pieces

- FRONT
- FRONT POCKET OVERLAY
- UPPER BACK
- NECK BAND
- UNDER CUFF
- GODET
- LOWER BACK
- UNDER COLLAR
- SLEEVE PLACKET
- SLEEVE

Pattern Alterations

Note the changes listed on page 54 of this book while following the pattern's instructions.

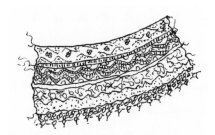

Layout and Construction

1 Fold the latticework. Cut the Front Pocket Overlay, Under Cuff, Godet, and Under Collar (figure 4).

2 Fold the sheet and cut the following: Front (two), Upper Back (two on fold—one is for lining), Lower Back (two), Sleeves (two), Under Cuff (two for lining), Under Collar (one on fold for lining), Neck Band (two on fold—one is for lining), and Sleeve Placket (eight—four are for lining).

3 Follow the pattern's instructions for construction, noting the alterations listed on page 54. Add lace to accent the cuffs and the hem of the upper back, as shown in the photo below.

Tip: Think creatively when you're searching for linens. The latticework in this blouse came from an old nightdress.

Pattern Courtesy of The Sewing Workshop: Chopin Blouse

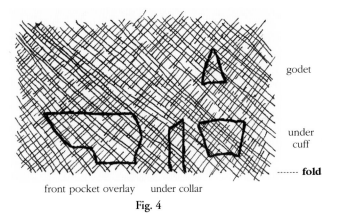

front pocket overlay   under collar

Fig. 4

Tea-Dyed Christening Gown with Antique Lace

This exquisite gown is embellished with antique laces and made using simplified heirloom sewing techniques.

You Will Need

- BASIC SEWING SUPPLIES

- 100 PERCENT COTTON SHEET, TEA-DYED TO MATCH THE LACE

- EXTRAFINE THREAD

- LACE AND SHEER TRIM FOR THE SLEEVES, COLLAR, AND HEM (SEVERAL YARDS OF EACH)

- ECRU GARMENT WITH TUCKS AND WIDE LACE (MEASURING AT LEAST 37 INCHES, THE CIRCUMFERENCE OF THE FINISHED GOWN)

- SNAPS

- SILK RIBBON

- SAFETY PIN

Pattern

- THE CHILDREN'S CORNER PATTERNS: HANDSEWING 1 (30)

Pattern Pieces

- JENNIFER: SLEEVE, FRONT, BACK

- MELISSA: COLLAR

- SLIP: FRONT, BACK

- CUSTOM PLACKET

- SLEEVE PLACKET

- BIAS

Note:

- PLEASE FOLLOW THE INSTRUCTIONS ON PAGE 62 TO CONSTRUCT THE GOWN. FOLLOW THE INSTRUCTIONS IN THE PATTERN ENVELOPE TO CONSTRUCT THE SLIP. USE EXTRAFINE THREAD AND ¼-INCH SEAM ALLOWANCES THROUGHOUT, UNLESS DIRECTED OTHERWISE.

Pattern Piece Alterations

Note the following changes before you cut the pieces out:

Neck Opening

I omitted the front opening and instead put a placket in the back. To incorporate this change, place the Center Front line of the Front on the fold when you're cutting out the pieces. Also, cut the following custom pieces: for the Placket, a strip that is 1½ x 16 inches; for the neck edge, a strip on the bias that is 1½ x 14 inches.

Long Sleeve Option

If you want a long Sleeve, add 4 inches to the short Sleeve and taper as shown in figure 1. Make custom Sleeve Plackets by cutting strips of fabric that are 1 x 7 inches for each edge.

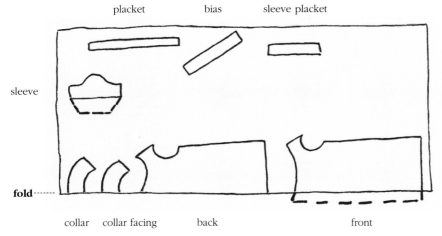

placket   bias   sleeve placket

sleeve

fold

collar   collar facing   back   front

Fig. 1

4 To construct the Placket in the back, see the instructions on page 22. Apply the Placket to the opening in the Back, but hand sew the Placket to the inside seam (figure 3). Fold under the left side of the Placket at the seamline so it lies on top of the right side.

5 Make the pleats in the Back by folding them toward the center, meeting at the Placket. Stitch across the neck edge to hold the pleats, but don't stitch along the folded edges of the pleats.

6 Stitch the shoulders in a French seam with wrong sides together, with the first seam ⅛ inch. Trim. Turn and stitch with the right sides together using a ⅛-inch seam allowance, encasing the previous seam. (See page 23 for more on using a French seam.)

7 To construct the short Sleeve, first transfer the markings to the sleeve. Then, gather the top of the Sleeve between the marks. Now, gather the bottom of the

Fig. 2

Fig. 3

Tea-Dyed Christening Gown with Antique Lace

Layout and Construction

1 Fold the dyed sheet and cut the Front, Back, Collar, Collar facing, Sleeve, Placket, Bias, and Sleeve Placket (figure 1 on page 61). Use the sheet again to cut the Slip Front and Slip Back, both on the fold. (See the instructions for tea dyeing on page 65.)

2 Mark the front pleats with a water-soluble marker. Fold the pleats on the solid line and stitch ⅛ inch from the edge. Press the pleats away from the center (figure 2).

3 Mark the back pleats, but wait to stitch them until after making the Placket.

Sleeve between the marks (figure 4). Trim the seam allowance on the Sleeve to ⅛ inch so it won't be visible through the sheer trim. Zigzag the raw edges. Place a piece of sheer trim on top of the seamline, wrong side of the trim to right side of the Sleeve, and zigzag the trim to bottom of Sleeve in a narrow stitch. Now, zigzag a piece of lace to the trim, using the edge-to-edge method (figure 5). Stitch the Sleeve into the armhole.

8 If you choose the long Sleeve option, gather the top and the bottom edges of the Sleeve as in step 7. Stitch the 1 x 7-inch Sleeve Placket to the bottom edge. Finish the strip at the bottom of the sleeve by turning it to the inside. Turn under the raw edge twice and slipstitch to the inside of Sleeve.

Fig. 4

Fig. 5

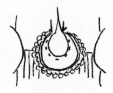

Fig. 6

9 Stitch the Collar pieces, right sides together. Trim, turn, and press. Apply a 20-inch piece of lace to the Collar edge using the edge-to-edge method. Staystitch the Collar to the neck edge, wrong side of the Collar to right side of Front and Back (figure 6). Remember that the opening is now in the back.

10 To finish the neck edge, pin the 1½ x 14-inch bias strip to the neck, right sides facing, leaving an extra ½ inch on each end. Stitch to the neck edge. Trim the seam to ⅛ inch. Turn the raw ends in and fold the strip in half. Press. Fold in half again to the inside of the neck edge, leaving a visible ⅛-inch neck edge. Pin the bias strip in place and whipstitch it to the inside.

11 Stitch the side and sleeve seams on one side only, right sides together (figure 7). Trim the seam to ⅛ inch and finish the raw edge with a zigzag stitch.

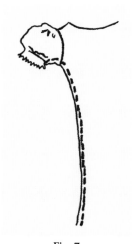

Fig. 7

12 To add the embellishments to the hem, first cut off the piece of the vintage garment you plan to use and open one side seam. (I used the elegant hem of a petticoat.) Finish the raw edge. The width of the piece of the vintage garment you use will determine how much to cut from the hem of the gown. Cut off the gown to the appropriate length and finish the raw edge with a tight zigzag stitch. Apply a 37-inch-long piece of trim to the finished edge of the gown, using the edge-to-edge method. Now, apply the vintage garment piece to the bottom edge of the trim, again using the edge-to-edge method.

13 Stitch the remaining side seam, right sides together.

14 To finish, sew a snap (or snaps) to the Placket. Tie a silk ribbon into a bow and fasten it to the collar from the inside, using a safety pin.

15 Refer to the instructions in the pattern envelope to construct the slip.

𝒯ip: I was fortunate enough to find a beautiful old petticoat with a hem that featured the tucks and the wide lace that I used in this project. You can add tucks and lace from different garments to re-create this look, of course, by stitching them together as described in step 12 above.

Variation: Gown with Handkerchief Collar

You Will Need

- BASIC SEWING SUPPLIES
- 100 PERCENT COTTON SHEET OR PURCHASED FABRIC
- EXTRAFINE THREAD
- ANTIQUE HANDKERCHIEF OR NAPKIN
- WIDE LACE
- SNAPS
- SILK RIBBON

Pattern

- THE CHILDREN'S CORNER PATTERNS: HANDSEWING 1 (30)

Pattern Pieces

- JENNIFER: FRONT, BACK, SLEEVE
- SLIP: FRONT, BACK
- CUSTOM PLACKET
- SLEEVE PLACKET
- BIAS

Note:

- USE EXTRAFINE THREAD AND ¼-INCH SEAM ALLOWANCES THROUGHOUT, UNLESS DIRECTED OTHERWISE.

Pattern Alterations

Follow the instructions for the Tea-Dyed Christening Gown with Antique Lace, pages 61-63. Use the long Sleeve option, but note the alteration for the Collar below.

Napkin or Handkerchief Collar

After you've completed step 2 on page 62 and made the pleats in the Front, insert this step. Lay the gown flat and place the napkin or handkerchief on top. Trace around the top edge of the dress with a water-soluble marker (figure 8). Cut out the collar along the lines you've just drawn. Pin it to the dress at the neck and armhole edges, wrong side of the collar to the right side of the dress (figure 9), and baste. Resume the instructions at step 3 on page 62, but omit step 9, as you've already attached the collar.

Layout and Construction

1. Follow the layout for the Tea-Dyed Christening Gown with Antique Lace (figure 1 on page 61), but omit the Collar.

2. Construct the garment per the instructions for the Tea-Dyed Christening Gown with Antique Lace, noting both the alterations listed on page 61 and the Collar alteration listed at the left.

Pattern Courtesy of The Children's Corner Patterns: Handsewing 1 (30)

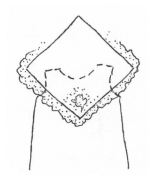

Fig. 8

Fig. 9

Tea Dyeing

Tea dyeing is a great way to make white fabric a lovely shade of ecru, and it will coordinate with many of the fine vintage laces in this color. Put five family-size tea bags in a big bowl and pour hot water over them. Let the tea brew until it's quite dark. Soak the fabric in the tea for a few minutes and then put it in the dryer to set the color. If it isn't dark enough, repeat the dyeing process. The colors don't have to be an exact match to be used together harmoniously.

Jacket with Fur Collar

A piece of vintage fur makes a luxe statement on a hip piece of outerwear.

You Will Need

- BASIC SEWING SUPPLIES
- LIGHTWEIGHT TRACING PAPER
- VINTAGE FUR COLLAR OR FUR PIECE
- STRETCH DENIM
- 2-INCH-WIDE ELASTIC
- 5 BUTTONS
- 2 SNAPS

Pattern

VOGUE PATTERNS 2730

Pattern Pieces

- FRONT
- FRONT FACING
- SIDE FRONT
- MIDDLE FRONT
- POCKET
- YOKE FRONT
- YOKE BACK
- BACK
- SIDE
- BAND
- COLLAR
- COLLAR BAND
- UPPER SLEEVE
- UNDER SLEEVE
- CUFF

Preparing the Fur

Before you begin to cut out this garment, turn the fur piece over and find the stitching that holds it together. (If you have a piece with appendages, simply cut them off.) Undo all the stitching until you're able to see the backing on the fur. Now, open the fur so it lies flat. Place the pattern piece on the fur (figure 1) and cut it out—don't worry, it won't shed much at all.

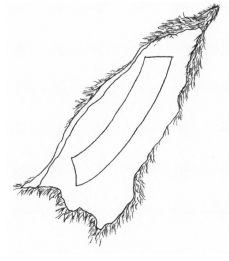

Fig. 1

Working with Fur

If the fur gets in your way while stitching the seams, tape it down and out of the way. If the finished collar and cuffs won't lie flat after clipping the curve, topstitch through the fur to hold it in place.

Pattern Alterations

Make these changes while following the instructions in the pattern envelope:

Collar

Take the Collar and make an adjusted pattern using the tracing paper. The original pattern piece comes to a point, which won't work well with the bulk of the fur. Alter the pattern to round it at the bottom (figure 2). Cut one Collar piece out of fur, and the other of stretch denim. (The fur is the right side of the Collar and the stretch denim is the Collar facing.) Follow the pattern instructions for constructing the Collar.

Cuff

Cut the Cuff pattern piece in half lengthwise (figure 3). Cut one Cuff out of stretch denim and one Cuff out of fur, adding a ⅝ inch seam allowance (figures 4 and 5). When you're assembling the Cuff, sew the two pieces together, right sides facing, with the fur as the outer Cuff. Stitch it to the garment per the pattern's instructions.

Layout and Construction

1 Follow the pattern's instructions for layout, using the stretch denim fabric except for the Collar and Cuff, as noted at the left.

2 Follow the pattern's instructions for construction, noting the alterations and tips listed at the left.

Fig. 2

Fig. 3

Fig. 4

Fig. 5

Variation: Vest with Fur Collar

You Will Need

- BASIC SEWING SUPPLIES
- VINTAGE FUR COLLAR OR FUR PIECE
- STRETCH CORDUROY
- 2-INCH WIDE ELASTIC
- ½-INCH SINGLE FOLD BIAS TAPE
- 5 BUTTONS

Pattern

- VOGUE PATTERNS 2730

Pattern Pieces

- FRONT
- FRONT FACING
- SIDE FRONT
- MIDDLE FRONT
- POCKET
- YOKE FRONT
- YOKE BACK
- BACK
- SIDE
- BAND
- COLLAR
- COLLAR BAND

Working with Fur

Note the suggestions for preparing and sewing with fur listed on page 67.

Pattern Alteration

Note the change listed for the Collar on page 67 of this book while following the pattern's instructions.

Layout and Construction

1   Follow the pattern's instructions for layout, using the stretch corduroy for all pieces except the Collar.

2   Follow the pattern's instructions for construction, noting the Collar alteration and tips listed on page 67.

Pattern Courtesy of The McCall Pattern Company: Vogue Patterns 2730

Charming Details...
Chenille, Cross-Stitch & More

Chenille Jacket

Create visual interest in this stylish jacket by careful placement of the pieces on the patterned chenille.

You Will Need

- BASIC SEWING SUPPLIES
- CHENILLE BEDSPREAD
- 4 BUTTONS

Pattern

- CUTTING LINE DESIGNS: BY POPULAR DEMAND #60565

Pattern Pieces

- FRONT
- BACK
- BACK YOKE
- COLLAR
- UPPER SLEEVE
- UNDER SLEEVE

Layout and Construction

1 Fold the chenille bedspread and place the pattern pieces to take advantage of its design (figure 1). In this project, the horizontal strips of chenille at the hem create the illusion of a band.

2 Follow the pattern's instructions for construction. The pockets and tabs were omitted in this project.

Pattern Courtesy of Cutting Line Designs: By Popular Demand #60565

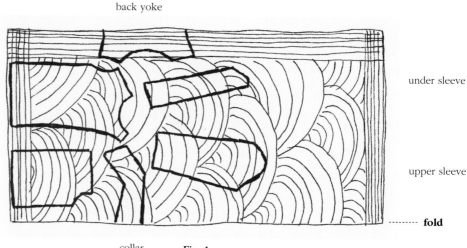

back yoke

front

under sleeve

upper sleeve

back

fold

collar **Fig. 1**

Graceful Cross-Stitch Dress

In addition to this cute dress, two variations follow, using a number of linens and featuring some construction alterations.

You Will Need

- BASIC SEWING SUPPLIES
- TABLECLOTH WITH CROSS-STITCH
- EXTRAFINE THREAD
- 3 SNAPS

Pattern

THE CHILDREN'S CORNER PATTERNS: GRACE

Pattern Pieces

- DRESS FRONT
- DRESS BACK
- COLLAR (OPTIONAL)
- SLEEVE B
- PLACKET
- BIAS

Note:

USE EXTRAFINE THREAD AND ¼-INCH SEAM ALLOWANCES THROUGHOUT, UNLESS DIRECTED OTHERWISE.

Pattern Alteration

Make this change while following the instructions in the pattern envelope:

Back Opening

The pattern calls for a middle pleat that's also the back opening, but I omitted it and made a regular placket instead. If you choose to do this also, you have to make this change when cutting out the fabric. Take the pleat out by folding the pattern in at the pleat mark before you cut, which leaves four pleats on either side (figure 1). To make the placket, see the instructions on page 22. Apply the placket to the opening in the back.

Layout and Construction

1 Fold the tablecloth; all the pattern pieces are cut from it. (I chose to include the Collar on this dress.) Place the Dress Front and Dress Back on the tablecloth so the cross-stitch is balanced on both sides of the dress, with the Collar and Sleeve cut from areas heavy with cross-stitch (figure 2). Note that the Collar piece is used as the lining piece, too, so cut four.

2 Follow the pattern's instructions for construction, noting the back opening alteration listed at the left.

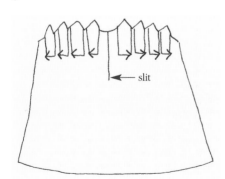

Fig. 1

bias placket sleeve lining

collar lining

collar

sleeve

dress back

dress front

fold

Fig. 2

You Will Need

- BASIC SEWING SUPPLIES
- SHEER LINEN TABLECLOTH WITH EMBROIDERY
- EXTRAFINE THREAD
- 3 SNAPS
- RIBBON

Pattern

- THE CHILDREN'S CORNER PATTERNS: GRACE

Pattern Pieces

- DRESS FRONT
- DRESS BACK
- PLACKET
- BIAS
- CUSTOM SLEEVE

Note:

USE EXTRAFINE THREAD AND ¼-INCH SEAM ALLOWANCES THROUGHOUT, UNLESS DIRECTED OTHERWISE.

Pattern Alterations

Note the change listed on page 72 of this book while following the pattern's instructions, as well as the Sleeve change listed below.

Sleeve (this variation only)

I made my own gathered Sleeve and lining for this variation. To use this custom Sleeve, enlarge the pattern to the dimensions shown, 14½ inches across and 4½ inches down (figure 3). To incorporate this change, stitch the Sleeve and Sleeve lining together along the long edge, right sides facing. Clip the seam, turn, and press. For gathers, make rows of long running stitches that are ⅛ inch and ¼ inch from the top edge of the Sleeve. Edgestitch the armhole ¼ inch from the outer edge. Pin the Sleeve to the armhole, pulling up the gathers to fit. Stitch. Trim the seam and clip the curves. Press the Sleeve out. Pin and stitch the Sleeve to the dress before you stitch the underarm seam.

Layout and Construction

1 Place the pattern pieces so two rows of embroidery embellish the Dress Front and Dress Back (figure 4). Place the Sleeve so it features embroidered flowers. Cut out the pattern pieces. (The Collar is omitted in this variation, and the neck edge is finished with Bias.)

2 Follow the pattern's instructions for construction, noting both the alteration listed on page 72 of this book and the Sleeve alteration listed at the left. Add a ribbon to finish, securing it on the wrong side of the fabric with a safety pin.

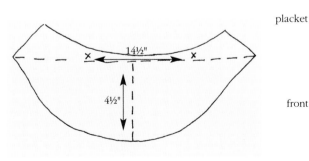

Fig. 3

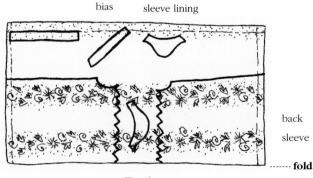

Fig. 4

Variation: Imitation Batiste Dress

You Will Need

- LINEN BRIDGE CLOTH WITH DECORATIVE EDGING
- IMITATION BATISTE
- EXTRAFINE THREAD
- 3 SNAPS

Pattern

- THE CHILDREN'S CORNER PATTERNS: GRACE

Pattern Pieces

- DRESS FRONT
- DRESS BACK
- COLLAR
- PLACKET
- BIAS
- SLEEVE

Note:

- USE EXTRAFINE THREAD AND ¼-INCH SEAM ALLOWANCES THROUGHOUT, UNLESS DIRECTED OTHERWISE.

Pattern Alteration

Note the change listed on page 72 of this book while following the pattern's instructions.

edging

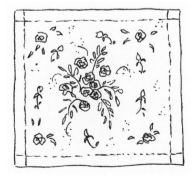

Fig. 5

Layout and Construction

1 Cut the Dress Front and Dress Back, Placket, and Bias from the imitation batiste.

2 This variation also features a hem decorated with the edging from the bridge cloth. To begin, cut away the edging from the bridge cloth (figure 5). Fold the bridge cloth, and cut the Collar and Sleeve from it (figure 6). Note that the Collar is used as the lining piece, too, so cut four.

3 Trim the edging you cut from the bridge cloth to 1½ inches wide. Stitch the pieces of the edging together to make one long continuous strip; finish the raw edge and press (figure 7).

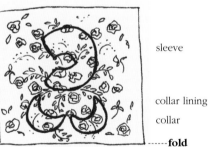

sleeve

collar lining
collar

-----**fold**

Fig. 6

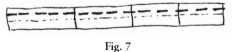

Fig. 7

Fig. 8

4 Follow the pattern's instructions for construction, noting the back opening alteration listed on page 72 of this book.

5 Add the decorative hem edging after making a 1-inch machine hem on the dress. Pin the hem edging strip to the dress 1 inch from the hemline, upside down and right sides together, extending the edging strip ½ inch beyond the side seam (figure 8). Stitch the hem edging strip to the dress. Next, stitch the ends of the edging together and finish the seam. Press down the edging.

Tip: You can easily incorporate small vintage pieces into your sewing, as shown in this dress; it's a charming result of combining small linens and purchased fabric.

Pattern Courtesy of The Children's Corner Patterns: Grace

Dress with Crocheted Yoke

The sweet lace on the yoke and sleeves of this dress add the finishing touch to a memorable garment for a special girl.

You Will Need

- BASIC SEWING SUPPLIES
- CROCHETED TABLE RUNNER OR SIMILAR TEXTILE
- IMITATION BATISTE, TO MATCH THE COLOR OF THE CROCHETED PIECE
- 3 SNAPS
- ½-INCH HEM TAPE, TO MATCH THE COLOR OF THE CROCHETED PIECE
- ¼-INCH ELASTIC
- SAFETY PIN

Pattern

- VOGUE PATTERNS 2105

Pattern Pieces

- FRONT
- BACK
- SLEEVE
- FRONT YOKE
- BACK YOKE
- PLACKET

Pattern Alteration

Make this change while following the pattern's instructions:

Sleeve

Before you stitch the underarm seam, gather the bottom of the Sleeve by making a casing from two strips of hem tape. First, pin the two strips of hem tape 1 inch from the bottom edge of each Sleeve, wrong sides together. (Since the hem tape matches the color of the crocheted piece, it will hardly be noticeable.) Stitch down the tape on both long edges (figure 1). Cut a strip of elastic and attach a small safety pin to the end. (I used about 8 inches of elastic for the sleeves on this size 6 dress.) Thread the elastic through the casing by pushing the safety pin, pinning the free end down if necessary. When the elastic is through the casing, remove the pin and stitch across each end. Stitch the underarm seam.

Layout and Construction

1 Fold the table runner. Cut the Front Yoke, Back Yoke, and Sleeve; place the bottom of the Sleeve on the edging of the table runner (figure 2).

2 Fold the imitation batiste and cut the Front, Back, Placket, and Yoke linings.

3 Follow the pattern's instructions for construction, noting the alterations listed at the left.

Tip: You can also use three crocheted place mats for the yokes and sleeves instead of the table runner.

Pattern Courtesy of The McCall Pattern Company: Vogue Patterns 2105

Fig. 1

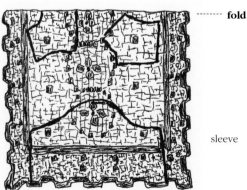

front yoke   back yoke

-------- **fold**

sleeve

Fig. 2

Holly Jolly Stockings

Have a little fun with some retro dishtowels and make these festive stockings for the holidays.

You Will Need

- BASIC SEWING SUPPLIES
- ARCHITECTURAL TRASH PAPER
- LINEN DISHTOWEL(S)
- FLEECE, TO MATCH DISHTOWEL(S)

Pattern

MCCALL'S CRAFT 2991

Pattern Pieces

- FRONT AND BACK
- CUFF
- TIE

Pattern Alterations

Make these changes while following the instructions in the pattern envelope:

Heel and Toe

Even though this pattern doesn't have separate heel and toe pieces, there are stitching lines for each drawn on the pattern pieces, so you can easily make the accent pieces I used in this project. Trace the heel and toe pieces onto architectural trash paper and cut them out as in step 2.

Layout and Construction

1 Lay the dishtowel flat and cut out one Front (figure 1).

2 Fold the remainder of the dishtowel and trace the Heel and Toe onto the fabric using a water-soluble marker. Cut out two of each Heel and Toe, as well as four Cuff pieces (figure 2).

3 Fold the fleece and cut out the following (figure 3): the Back for the stocking you cut in step 1; the remaining Front and Back (two); Cuff (four); and Tie (two).

4 Follow the pattern's instructions for the construction of each stocking. To add the Heel and Toe, appliqué them on both sides of the stocking before sewing it together.

Tip: Make two different versions of the stocking for a delightfully mismatched pair, as in this project.

Pattern Courtesy of The McCall Pattern Company: McCall's Craft 2991

front (cut 1)

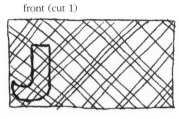

Fig. 1

cuff

cuff lining

toe

heel

----- **fold**

Fig. 2

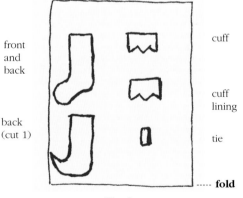

front and back

back (cut 1)

cuff

cuff lining

tie

----- **fold**

Fig. 3

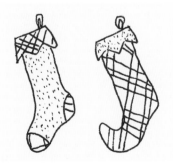

Chenille Sofa Cushions

Bring new life to a chenille bedspread—and your living room—by re-covering your sofa cushions.

You Will Need

Layout and Construction

1 Measure the top of your existing cushion and add ⅝ inch around all the edges for the seam allowance. Make a custom pattern piece out of the tracing paper to these measurements; this will be the Top and Bottom of the cushion (figure 1). Place the pattern piece on the chenille, considering the design placement on the Top, and cut out the Top of each cushion. You may need to cut each piece separately to match the design motifs in your chenille. Use the same pattern piece to cut out the Bottom, but use the cotton duck.

2 To add the zipper, first measure the depth of your cushion and add 2½ inches to this measurement. Now, add 3¼ inches to the length of your zipper, and cut one strip from the cotton duck to these measurements. (For example, in this project, the depth of the cushion was 5 inches; the additional 2½ inches made this measurement 7½ inches. The zipper was 30 inches long; the additional 3¼ inches made this measurement 33¼ inches. So the strip was cut to 7½ x 33¼ inches.)

3 Cut the strip in half lengthwise (figure 2) and finish the inside edges. Turn these finished edges under ⅝ inch and press down. Pin the zipper under these two pieces, centered lengthwise, and stitch with a zipper foot. Stitch across the top and the bottom of the zipper (figure 3).

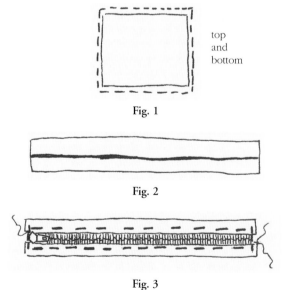

top
and
bottom

Fig. 1

Fig. 2

Fig. 3

Chenille Sofa Cushions

4 The depth of your strip should now equal the depth of your cushion plus ⅝ inch on either side for the seam allowance. Cut a strip (or strips) this depth from the cotton duck until the length equals the circumference of your cushion plus 2 inches. Sew the strips together if necessary, but leave the end open (figure 4). (You'll stitch this seam in the next step.) This is the boxing strip for the cushion.

5 Pin the boxing strip to the chenille Top, right sides together. Where the ends meet, pin and stitch them together. Stitch the boxing strip to the Top.

6 To add the Bottom, unzip the zipper, turn the cushion inside out, and pin the Bottom to the boxing strip, right sides together (figure 5). Stitch the seam and turn the cushion right side out, pulling it through the opened zipper.

Alternative: If you're lucky enough to have a large piece of chenille, you can make the entire cushions from chenille, of course.

Fig. 4

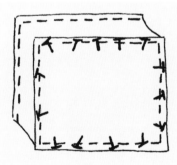

Fig. 5

Toddler Jacket and Hat

Bundle up your baby with style in these darling jackets, one with a matching hat. Both variations are made from cutter quilts.

You Will Need

- BASIC SEWING SUPPLIES
- CUTTER QUILT
- MEDIUM-WEIGHT LINING FABRIC
- 3 VINTAGE BUTTONS
- WIDE RIBBON, IN A MATCHING COLOR

Pattern

- VOGUE PATTERNS 7628

Pattern Pieces

- JACKET: FRONT, BACK, COLLAR, SLEEVE
- HAT: BRIM, CROWN, FLAP, TOP

Toddler Jacket and Hat

Working with Damaged Quilts

Please, never cut a vintage quilt in good condition. They should be preserved. But you can always find damaged quilts (called cutters) and work with the portions of them that are still in good shape. To use a cutter quilt, open it and place the pattern where the design looks appealing. If the area of the quilt you like has just one bad spot, you can sometimes repair it by stitching with a zigzag stitch. You can also replace badly damaged spots with fabric pieces from another place on the quilt; again, use a zigzag stitch and simply stitch the replacement fabric piece on top of the bad spots. If you don't want the stitches to show, use invisible thread.

Pattern Alterations

Make these changes while following the instructions in the pattern envelope:

Front Facing

Rather than face the front of these jackets, I used the decorative edging on the quilts for the front edges. (You can also do this for the bottom of a sleeve or a hem.) If the facing is part of the pattern piece and you don't want or don't need it, cut it off the pattern piece or use the facing line as the cutting line, as I did here.

Cuffs

Omit the cuffs from both jackets.

Layout and Construction

1 Fold the quilt and place the jacket Front, Sleeve, Collar, and Back, and hat Top, Flap, Brim, and Crown pieces as shown (figure 1). Cut out the pieces.

2 Cut the Flap, Brim, and Collar linings from the folded lining fabric.

3 Follow the pattern's instructions for construction, noting the alterations listed at the left.

Tip: I love making children's jackets and hats out of old quilts because they're so colorful and warm, and the jackets are easy to make. You can probably find severely damaged quilts that have salvageable pieces large enough for children's clothing. Some of the pieces may need to be mended, but they're usually stable after doing so. They make truly charming garments, don't they?

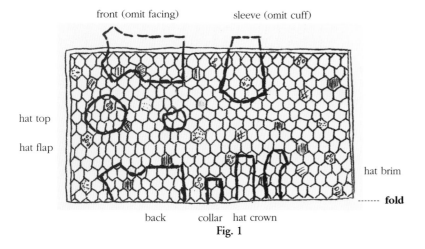

Fig. 1

Variation: Scalloped Edge Jacket

You Will Need
- CUTTER QUILT WITH DECORATIVE EDGING
- LINING FABRIC
- 1 VINTAGE BUTTON

Pattern
- VOGUE PATTERNS 7628

Pattern Pieces
- FRONT
- BACK
- SLEEVE
- CUSTOM FRONT AND BACK NECK FACING

Working with Damaged Quilts
Please note the paragraph on page 86 about working with damaged quilts.

Pattern Alterations
Note the changes listed on page 86 of this book while following the pattern's instructions, as well as the changes listed below.

Collar and Neck Facing
Omit the collar and apply a neck facing. You don't need the entire Front facing since you're using the decorative edge of the quilt for the Front edge. But you do need to make a separate Neck Facing, using the neck portion of the Front facing and the neckline of the Back (figures 2 and 3). Simply draw in a

facing on these pieces, transferring it to paper if necessary, and cut out. The facing you make for the Back should be cut on the fold.

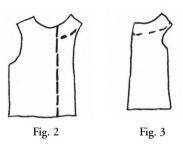

Fig. 2   Fig. 3

Layout and Construction

1   Follow the layout for the Toddler Jacket (figure 1 on page 86), noting both the alterations listed on that page and the alterations listed at the left; omit the Hat pieces and the Collar. Cut the Neck Facing pieces from lining fabric. Remember that you're placing the Front on the edge and won't incorporate the facing portion of the Front pattern piece.

2   Follow the pattern's instructions for construction, noting both the alterations listed on page 86 of this book and the alterations listed at the left. Add the facing at the Collar step: Stitch the Front and Back facings together, right sides facing, and then finish the raw edge. Stitch the facing to the neck edge, right sides together, trim the seam, and clip the curves. Turn the facing to the inside and tack in place.

Pattern Courtesy of The McCall Pattern Company: Vogue Patterns 7628

Cosmopolitan Cross-Stitch Jacket

This stylish jacket is easy to make, and an artsy placement on the fabric is all you need to create a unique garment.

You Will Need

- LARGE TABLECLOTH WITH CROSS-STITCH
- 2 LARGE VINTAGE BUTTONS

Pattern

- THE SEWING WORKSHOP: SAN DIEGO JACKET

Pattern Pieces

- FRONT
- BACK
- SLEEVE FRONT
- SLEEVE BACK

Layout and Construction

1. Fold the tablecloth and place the pattern pieces so the cross-stitch runs down the Front and the Sleeve Front. Place the Back on the fold as shown (figure 1). Cut out the pieces.

2. Follow the pattern's instructions for construction. As a finishing detail, I chose to leave off the button loops and instead make two buttonholes across the top of the jacket.

Tip: I love the construction of this jacket because it has no separate facing pieces. But you should choose a pretty fabric for this garment because this construction doesn't allow for a contrasting facing.

Pattern Courtesy of The Sewing Workshop: San Diego Jacket

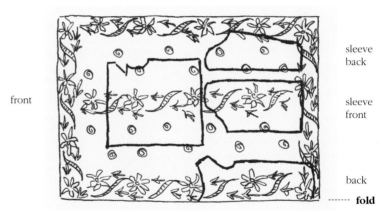

Fig. 1

Fabulous Footstool Cover

These busy barkcloth prints were all the rage in the 1950s, with fanciful geometric shapes and intriguing color combinations.

You Will Need

- BASIC SEWING SUPPLIES
- LIGHTWEIGHT TRACING PAPER
- BARKCLOTH DRAPES OR YARDAGE
- 3 BUTTONS, IN A MATCHING COLOR

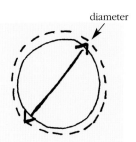

Fig. 1

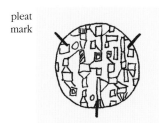

Fig. 2

Fig. 3

Layout and Construction

1 To make a cover for a round footstool, begin by measuring the diameter and make a custom pattern piece for the Top, adding a ½-inch seam allowance (figure 1).

2 To determine the size of the Skirt, measure the height of the footstool and add an additional 1½ inches to allow for a ½ seam and a 1 inch hem. To calculate the width needed for the Skirt, begin with the circumference of the stool and add 12 inches for each pleat. Factor in a ½-inch seam allowance. I designed this cover to have three pleats, so I added 36 inches to the circumference. (For example, in this project, the height of the stool was 17 inches, so I added the extra 1½ inches to have a total length of 18½ inches. The circumference of the stool was 56 inches; I added 36 inches for the three pleats and I added 1 inch for the seam allowances to yield a width of 93 inches.)

3 Use the custom pattern piece from step 1 and the measurements from step 2 to cut your fabric. You may have to cut separate pieces and sew them together to reach the desired width for your Skirt—if you're piecing the fabric together, remember to add a ½-inch seam allowance for each seam you need.

4 Use a water-soluble marker to mark where you want the pleats to fall, spacing them evenly around the footstool (figure 2). Pin the Skirt to the Top, right sides together, making inverted pleats as you go by folding the fabric over on itself to a depth of 3 inches on both sides of the mark, the folds meeting at the mark. (Each side of the pleat uses 6 inches of fabric.) Stitch the Skirt to the Top in a ½-inch seam.

5 Make a 1-inch machine hem. Sew a button on each pleat, 5 inches from the top (figure 3).

Market Bag

Take this one-of-a-kind tote with you on every shopping trip. Accent this bag with colorful piping.

You Will Need

- BASIC SEWING SUPPLIES
- LINEN TABLE RUNNER WITH PRINTS ON EACH END
- 100 PERCENT COTTON SHEET
- PIPING, TO MATCH THE TABLE RUNNER (OPTIONAL)
- WEBBING, TO MATCH THE TABLE RUNNER (OPTIONAL)

Pattern

VOGUE PATTERNS 7726

Pattern Pieces

- FRONT AND BACK
- SIDE

Layout and Construction

1 Cut the Front lining, Back lining, Side, and Side lining from the folded sheet. Lay the table runner flat to cut out the Front and Back; you'll have to cut each piece separately (figure 1).

2 Follow the pattern's instructions for Purse A, omitting the pocket. I added the piping, as well as a handle made from webbing instead of fabric.

Pattern Courtesy of The McCall Pattern Company: Vogue Patterns 7726

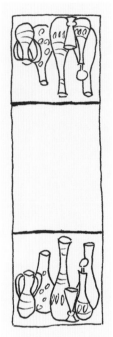

front

back

Fig. 1

Quilted Chair Cap

Dress up your wicker or rattan chair with a
delightful cap salvaged from damaged quilts.

You Will Need

- BASIC SEWING SUPPLIES

- LIGHTWEIGHT TRACING PAPER

- LARGE CUTTER QUILT(S)

- ½-INCH SINGLE FOLD BIAS TAPE, IN A MATCHING COLOR

Working with Damaged Quilts

Please, never cut a vintage quilt in good condition. They should be preserved. But you can always find damaged quilts (called cutters) and work with the portions of them that are still in good shape. To use a cutter quilt, open it and place the pattern where the design looks appealing. If the area of the quilt you like has just one bad spot, you can sometimes repair it by stitching with a zigzag stitch. You can also replace badly damaged spots with fabric pieces from another place on the quilt; again, use a zigzag stitch and simply stitch the replacement fabric piece on top of the bad spots. If you don't want the stitches to show, use invisible thread.

Layout and Construction

1 Begin by measuring the chair across the top and down the arms to the length you want to cover with the cap. Measure the width of the chair at this spot. (For example, in this project, the top and arm measurement was 48 inches; the length was 13 inches; and the width was 38 inches. See figure 1.) Transfer these measurements to the tracing paper and

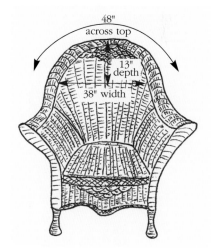

Fig. 1

Quilted Chair Cap

make your own custom pattern piece, adding a ½-inch seam allowance all around (figure 2).

2 To make the boxing strip, measure the depth of the chair at the side, taking into account any decorative features the arms of your chair may have. Add a ½-inch seam allowance on each side. This measurement is the width of the boxing strip. Use the top and arm measurement from step 1 for the length of the boxing strip, adding 4 inches. (For example, in this project, the depth of the chair was 4 inches and the top measurement was 48 inches, so the boxing strip was cut to 5 x 52 inches.)

3 Cut one Front and one Back separately, and cut one piece for the boxing strip (figure 3). Zigzag or serge the raw edges on each piece.

cap

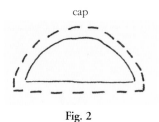

Fig. 2

4 Stitch the boxing strip to the Front, right sides together. Now, stitch the other side of the boxing strip to the Back, right sides together. Trim the excess from the boxing strip so it's even with the Front and the Back pieces (figure 4). Finish the raw edges.

5 Open the bias tape and stitch it to the bottom edge of the chair cap. Turn the binding to the inside and stitch.

boxing strip

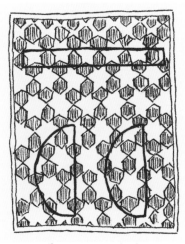

Fig. 4

front **Fig. 3** back

Timeless Textiles...
Florals, Stripes & More

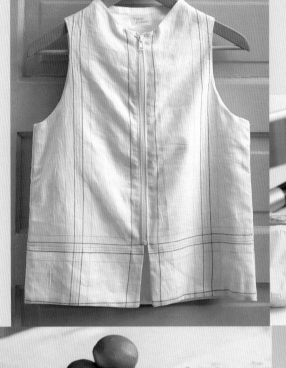

Purse with Faux Tortoiseshell Handles

Here's a charming accessory for the lover of vintage fabrics; this purse also features vintage handles.

You Will Need

- BASIC SEWING SUPPLIES
- LIGHTWEIGHT TRACING PAPER
- LINEN WITH APPLIQUÉ OR EMBROIDERY
- LINING FABRIC (OPTIONAL)
- MEDIUM-WEIGHT INTERFACING
- PIPING, IN A CONTRASTING COLOR
- PURSE HANDLES

front and back

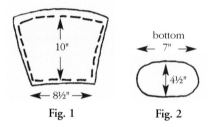

Fig. 1   **Fig. 2**

bottom lining   bottom

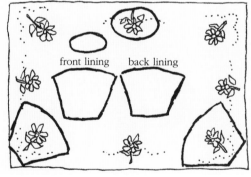

front   **Fig. 3**   back

Layout and Construction

1 Make the custom pattern pieces from the tracing paper, using the measurements supplied in figures 1 and 2. You need to make pattern pieces for the Front and Back, as well as the Bottom.

2 Cut one Front, one Back, and one Bottom from the vintage linen, centering the pieces on the appliqué or embroidery (figure 3). For the purse lining, cut another Front, Back, and Bottom out of the undecorated portion of the linen. (You can also use lining fabric for these pieces, if desired.) Lastly, cut one Front, one Back, and one Bottom out of the interfacing.

3 Apply the interfacing to the purse pieces. Stitch the Front and the Back together at the sides, right sides facing (figure 4). Stitch the Front and Back linings in the same manner.

4 Staystitch the Bottom and notch the curves (figure 5). Pin and stitch the Bottom to the Front and Back, right sides together. Pin and stitch the Bottom lining to the Front and Back lining in the same manner.

5 Use a zipper foot to stitch the piping to the top edge of the purse, right sides together, with the piping upside down (figure 6).

6 Turn the purse inside out and insert the lining into the purse, right sides together. Pin the lining to the top edge of the purse and stitch with a zipper foot, leaving a 3-inch opening. Pull the purse and lining through the opening, turning the purse right side out. Push the lining back into the purse. Press. Whipstitch the opening closed.

7 Follow the manufacturer's instructions to attach the handles.

Tip: I was lucky enough to find an old purse at a flea market and I removed the handles to use in this project. Always keep your eyes open for vintage items you can incorporate in your sewing; you never know when you might find a treasure.

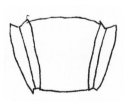

Fig. 4

Fig. 5

Fig. 6

Tulip Yoke Dress

Made from a great pattern that can be used over and over again as a jumper or sundress, this project features some cheerful appliqué and embroidery.

You Will Need

BASIC SEWING SUPPLIES

100 PERCENT COTTON SHEET

1 OR 2 LINENS WITH EMBROI-
DERY AND/OR APPLIQUÉ; THE
COLORS SHOULD COORDINATE
IF YOU USE 2 DIFFERENT
LINENS (A TABLECLOTH AND
TABLE RUNNER WERE USED IN
THIS PROJECT)

3 VINTAGE BUTTONS

Pattern

THE CHILDREN'S CORNER
PATTERNS: LOUISE

Pattern Pieces

SKIRT FRONT

SKIRT BACK

BACK YOKE

BACK YOKE LINING

FRONT YOKE

FRONT YOKE LINING

Layout and Construction

1 Cut out all the pattern pieces from the folded cotton sheet *except* the Back Yoke.

2 Open the Front Yoke and place it on top of the appliquéd tablecloth. Make sure the appliqué is straight. Draw the outline of the Front Yoke onto the linen, using a water-soluble marker. Draw a simple patch pocket around the other appliqué (figure 1). Cut out these pieces.

Fig. 1

3 Pin the appliqué to the Front Yoke, wrong side of the appliqué on the right side of the Front Yoke, and stitch it on all edges, making it part of the Front Yoke. (Yes, you've appliquéd the appliqué to the Front Yoke!)

4 Lay the table runner flat and separately cut out each side of the Back Yoke from the embroidered ends (figure 2).

5 Follow the pattern's instructions for construction.

Tip: This dress is a good example of how to use your imagination and think in terms of elements when designing with vintage linens. I had a very small, square, white tablecloth that had appliquéd tulips on two corners, and I thought it would be perfect in a child's dress. So, I found a pattern that featured a front yoke, and I decided to use one of the appliquéd corners as the yoke. I had an embroidered table runner in my linen collection that matched the colors in the tulips, so I used it for the back yoke (see below). Then, I incorporated the remaining tulip into a pocket and added it to the front. You can use just about any size or shape linen if you find a pattern that contains the right elements. You can even add an entirely new piece, like the pocket on this dress.

back yoke   back yoke

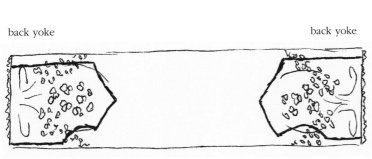

Fig. 2

Variation: Bordered Tablecloth Dress

You Will Need

- BASIC SEWING SUPPLIES
- TABLECLOTH WITH A LARGE BORDER
- LINING FABRIC
- 3 VINTAGE BUTTONS

Pattern

THE CHILDREN'S CORNER PATTERNS: LOUISE

Pattern Pieces

- SKIRT FRONT
- SKIRT BACK
- BACK YOKE
- BACK YOKE LINING
- FRONT YOKE
- FRONT YOKE LINING

Pattern Alteration

(this variation only)
Make this change while following the instructions in the pattern envelope:

Pleats

Omit the pleats in this dress. To remove the pleats, fold the pattern piece in at the pleat mark before you cut.

Layout and Construction

1 Fold the tablecloth and place the Skirt Front and Skirt Back pieces on the fold, with the bottom of the skirt falling on the border. You'll have to place the pattern pieces on separate ends of the cloth to do this (figure 3). Be sure the borders match up at the side seams before you cut.

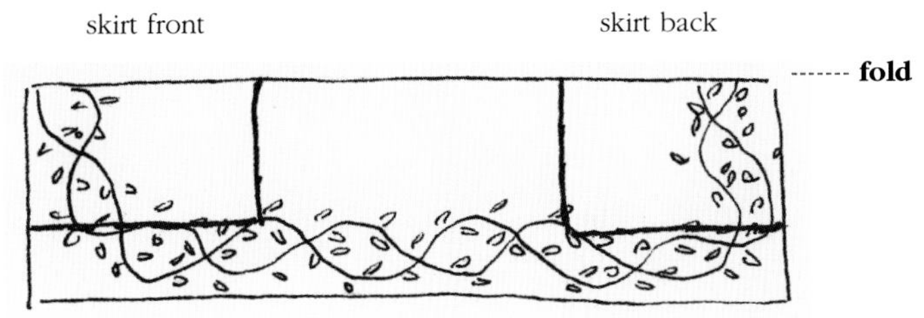

skirt front   skirt back   ----- **fold**

Fig. 3

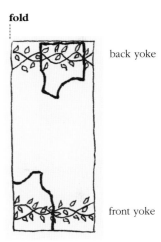

2 After cutting out the skirt pieces, fold the leftover cloth to cut the yokes, placing the Front Yoke on the fold (figure 4). This allows you to take advantage of the design on the border, so be sure to carefully place the yokes on the tablecloth. (I especially love the way this border looks on the Front Yoke of this project.)

3 Cut the Front Yoke Lining and the Back Yoke Lining from the lining material.

fold

back yoke

front yoke

Fig. 4

4 Follow the pattern's instructions for construction, noting the pleat alteration listed at the left.

Tip: Omitting the pleats not only allows you to use less material, but it also lets you emphasize a pretty border or edging, like the one in this project. If you made pleats in this border, it would ruin the symmetry of the linen's design motif.

Pattern Courtesy of The Children's Corner Patterns: Louise

Vintage Miniskirt

The bold eye-catching patterns in this skirt
are great for a fun-loving teenager.

You Will Need

BASIC SEWING SUPPLIES

LARGE TABLECLOTH

ZIPPER

Pattern

MCCALLS 3501

Pattern Pieces

FRONT

BACK

FRONT FACING

BACK FACING

CUSTOM RUFFLE

Layout and Construction

1 Study the design of your tablecloth and decide how you can best incorporate it into the skirt. In this project, I folded the tablecloth and placed the Back and the Front in opposite directions so the side seams would match (figure 1). Place the Front Facing, Back Facing, and optional Ruffle as well, and cut out all the pieces.

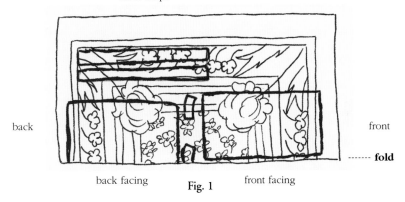

Fig. 1

2 Follow the pattern's instructions for construction. I added the cute ruffle at the hem. The length of the ruffle should be twice the circumference of the bottom of the skirt. To make the ruffle, cut strips from the tablecloth that are 2½ inches wide and sew them together to the length you need. Serge or zigzag one edge of the ruffle, turn it under ¼ inch, and stitch (figure 2). Gather the top edge of the ruffle with two lines of long running stitches. Sew the ruffle to the bottom edge of the skirt using a ¼-inch seam allowance, starting and ending at a side seam. Be sure to check the length of the skirt before you apply the ruffle.

Pattern Courtesy of The McCall Pattern Company: McCalls 3501

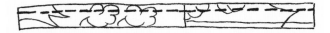

Fig. 2

Atomic Café Curtains

This lively mid-century tablecloth had a border
that translated into excellent café curtains.

You Will Need

- BASIC SEWING SUPPLIES

- TABLECLOTH WITH GRAPHIC DESIGN MOTIFS

- 100 PERCENT COTTON SHEET OR LINING FABRIC

- DECORATIVE CURTAIN HANGERS

Layout and Construction

1 First, measure your window. The curtain needs to be double the width of the window and about 12 or 13 inches in length.

2 Now, study the design of the tablecloth and decide how to best use it in the curtains. This tablecloth had a border about 13 inches wide that was perfect for the length of the curtain, so I cut the border to use in this project (figure 1).

3 Cut out the curtains to the desired width; you'll probably have to sew some pieces together to reach the desired measurement (figure 2). After cutting off the border, I had 122 inches of fabric in two long pieces and two short pieces. For a large window, sew all four pieces together. For a small window, sew one short piece and one long piece together.

4 Cut the lining to the same measurements you used for the curtain, using an old sheet or lining fabric. Place the pieces right sides together and stitch, leaving an opening to turn (figure 3).

5 Turn and press. Stitch the opening closed. Make buttonholes across the top, 3 inches apart (figure 4).

Tip: In addition to café hangers, the hardware used for hanging shower curtains is great for this project. There's a lot of variety on the market now, so you'll have no trouble finding just the right hardware to complement your vintage linen.

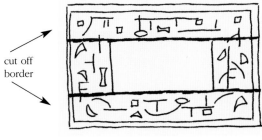

cut off border

Fig. 1

Fig. 2

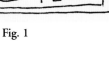

Fig. 3

buttonholes

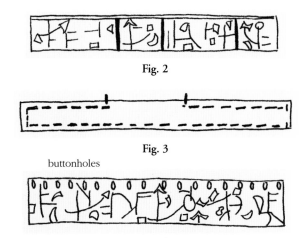

Fig. 4

Blooming Rose Boudoir Set

Safeguard your precious belongings with these nostalgic accessories made from a romantic print.

You Will Need

- BASIC SEWING SUPPLIES
- MEDIUM-SIZE VINTAGE LINEN
- VINTAGE RIBBON AND/OR LACE, TO COORDINATE WITH THE LINEN

Pattern

- MCCALL'S CRAFT 4073

Pattern Pieces

- GARMENT SHOULDER GUARD
- COSMETIC BAG

Layout and Construction

1 Place the pattern pieces on the fabric to best display its design features. Here, a border of flowers is perfect along the bottom of the shoulder guard (figure 1). Cut out the pieces.

2 Follow the instructions in the pattern envelope for making B, Garment Shoulder Guard, and E, Cosmetic Bag. Add lace and ribbon embellishments as desired (figure 2).

Pattern Courtesy of The McCall Pattern Company: McCall's Craft 4073

cosmetic bag

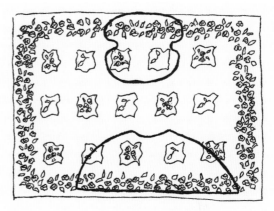

garment shoulder guard

Fig. 1

Fig. 2

Fitted Tablecloth with Lace Trim

Create your own tailored tablecloth by fitting an existing vintage piece to your favorite table—great for alfresco dining, too.

You Will Need

- BASIC SEWING SUPPLIES

- SQUARE OR RECTANGULAR TABLECLOTH, LARGE ENOUGH TO HANG A FEW INCHES OVER THE SIDES OF YOUR TABLE

- EXTRAFINE OR INVISIBLE THREAD

- VINTAGE LACE, TO MATCH THE TABLECLOTH (ENOUGH TO GO AROUND THE CIRCUMFERENCE OF THE TABLE)

Layout and Construction

1 Center the design of the tablecloth in the middle of your table and decide how much you want to hang over the edge. (This project drapes about 5 inches over the edge.) Cut off the excess fabric all around and finish the edges by using a zigzag stitch or a serger. Put the tablecloth back on the table, wrong side up, and pin the corners together to fit the edge of the table (figure 1).

2 Stitch the corners. Trim the seam and press. Stitch the lace to the edge of the tablecloth using extrafine or invisible thread and a zigzag stitch, placing the lace over the finished raw edge (figure 2).

Tip: In addition to creating a custom look for your dining table, this is also a good way to use a vintage tablecloth that may be tattered around the edges. The lace revives the beauty of the original piece.

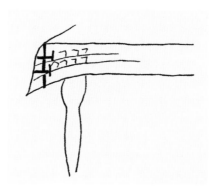

Fig. 1

Fig. 2

Simple Sleeveless Top

Bold fruit graphics from a vintage tablecloth add pizzazz to the chic modern styling of this top.

You Will Need

- TABLECLOTH WITH FRUIT OR FLOWER MOTIFS

- LINING FABRIC

- ZIPPER

Pattern

VOGUE 2491

Pattern Pieces

FRONT

BACK

See this variation on page 114.

Layout and Construction

1 Fold the tablecloth and place the pattern pieces (figure 1). Cut them out. Use the Front and Back pieces to cut out the lining, too.

2 Follow the pattern's instructions for construction.

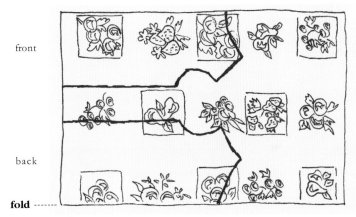

Fig. 1

Variation: Striped Top

Layout and Construction

1 Fold the tablecloth and place the pattern pieces (figure 2), matching the stripes. Cut out the pieces. Use the Front and Back pieces to cut out the lining, too.

2 Follow the pattern's instructions for construction.

Pattern Courtesy of The McCall Pattern Company: Vogue Patterns 2491

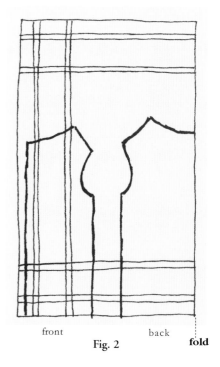

front   back   **fold**

Fig. 2

You Will Need
- TABLECLOTH WITH STRIPED BORDERS
- LINING FABRIC
- ZIPPER

Pattern
- VOGUE 2491

Pattern Pieces
- FRONT
- BACK

Striped Pillow with Beads

Embellish an ordinary pillow with triangles of
vintage linen and sparkling bead accents.

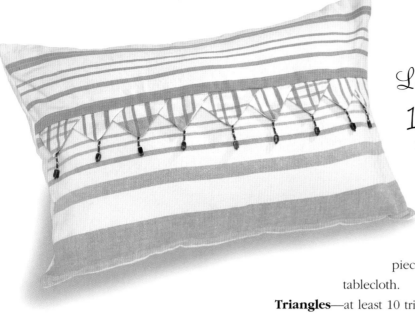

Layout and Construction

1 Lay the tablecloth flat. Cut the following pieces (figure 1):

Front—two pieces from the tablecloth that have stripes running lengthwise. One piece should be 9 x 20 inches and the other 6 x 20 inches.

Back—two pieces that are each 14 x 24 inches. Use the sheeting for these Back pieces if you don't have enough of the striped tablecloth.

Triangles—at least 10 triangles at the intersection of the horizontal and vertical stripes, and at least 10 triangles of lining anywhere on the tablecloth. (You may need more, or fewer, than 10 depending on how you overlap them.) Use the template in figure 2, enlarging it 200 percent.

2 To make each triangle, place one string of beads upside down and pin it into the point of the triangle. Put the triangle and its lining piece right sides together with the bead string in between them. Stitch around the edges using a ¼-inch seam allowance, but leave the top open. Turn and press (figure 3).

3 Take the 6 x 20-inch Front piece and place the triangles upside down on the bottom edge, right sides facing, overlapping each triangle with the adjacent one. I used only nine triangles because that

You Will Need

BASIC SEWING SUPPLIES

STRIPED TABLECLOTH

100 PERCENT COTTON OR LINEN SHEET (OPTIONAL)

STANDARD BED PILLOW, ALTERED AS BELOW

AT LEAST 10 STRINGS OF BEADS

Note:

THE 13 X 19-INCH PILLOW USED IN THIS PROJECT IS A CUSTOM SIZE. TO GET THIS NICE REC-TANGULAR SIZE, I USED A STAN-DARD BED PILLOW AND REMOVED SOME OF THE STUFF-ING. THIS IS A GOOD TRICK FOR CUSTOMIZING A PILLOW!

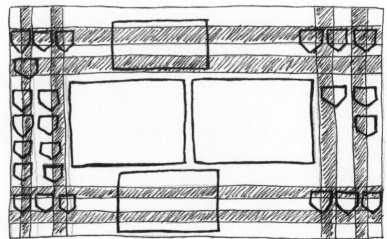

front, 6" x 20"

triangles

back, 14" x 24" (cut 2)

triangles

front, 9" x 20"

Fig. 1

arrangement appealed to me, so use your judgement when you're overlapping the triangles. Stitch using a ¼-inch seam allowance (figure 4).

4 Place the 9 x 20-inch Front piece on top of the piece with the triangles, right sides together, and stitch using a ½-inch seam allowance. Stitch the seam again. Press the triangles down and topstitch (figure 5).

5 Take the Back pieces and fold them in half to yield two pieces that are 14 x 12 inches. With right sides together, place one of the Back pieces on the left side of the Front, raw edges even and the fold in the middle. Now, place the other piece on the right side of the Front, also matching raw edges. They will overlap in the middle, and this will serve as the opening to insert your pillow form. Stitch around the pillow using a ½-inch seam allowance. Trim the seam, turn, and press. Insert the pillow. (The construction described in this step was illustrated in the Linen Napkin Pillow project on page 30, figure 3).

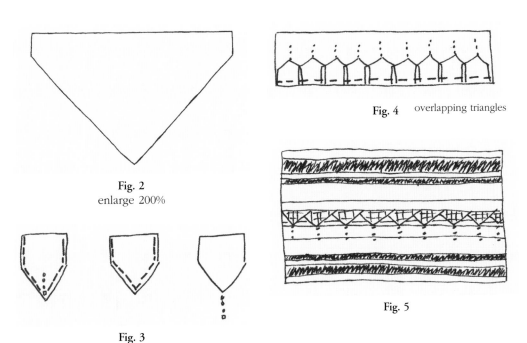

Fig. 2
enlarge 200%

Fig. 3

Fig. 4   overlapping triangles

Fig. 5

Curtains with Checked Borders

A great use for cotton sheets, these curtains feature borders and ties from a cheery tablecloth.

You Will Need

- BASIC SEWING SUPPLIES
- 100 PERCENT COTTON SHEET(S)
- CHECKED TABLECLOTH
- DECORATIVE CURTAIN HANGERS

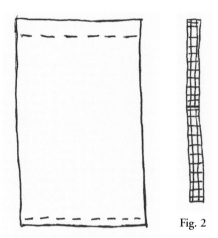

Fig. 1

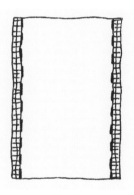

Fig. 3

Fig. 4

Layout and Construction

1 Begin by measuring the width of your window(s). This will determine how many sheets you need. The width of your curtain should be double the width of your window. After figuring the width, measure the length you need; add 2 inches at the top for a casing and 1 inch at the bottom for a hem. Cut the Curtain to these measurements (figure 1). To make the casing, turn under ¼ inch at the top and stitch. Turn under 1¾ inches and stitch again.

2 To create the side edging from the tablecloth, cut strips the length of your curtain by 2 inches wide. Sew strips together to reach the length, if necessary (figure 2). Finish one raw edge along the length of each edging.

3 Stitch the edging to both long edges of the Curtain in a ⅜-inch seam, right sides and unfinished edges together. Press the border away from the Curtain. Fold the edging over the seam to the inside. Stitch "in the ditch" (along the seamline) through all layers to finish (figure 3). This seam finish gives the edging stability.

4 Cut the bottom border from the tablecloth; it should be 13 inches long by the width of your Curtain. Mark a stitching line on the Curtain that's 11½ inches from the bottom. Place the tablecloth border upside down along this seamline, right sides together, and stitch using a ½-inch seam allowance. Press the border down. Fold the sides of the border under and whipstitch to the side edgings. Make a 1-inch machine hem.

5 To finish, make buttonholes along the top that are 3 inches apart. Cut decorative strips from the tablecloth that are 1 x 10 inches. Finish the raw edges with a tight zigzag stitch. Mark the center of each tie and stitch them to the curtain at these marks, placing a tie below each buttonhole (figure 4). Tie in a bow or a knot as desired. Hang using decorative curtain hardware.

buttonholes   ties

Porch Swing Cushion

Spend a lazy afternoon in the swing with a comfy cushion made from a vintage tablecloth.

You Will Need

- BASIC SEWING SUPPLIES
- LIGHTWEIGHT TRACING PAPER
- TABLECLOTH
- BATTING, STUFFING, OR FOAM CUSHION
- UPHOLSTERY ZIPPER, ABOUT 6 INCHES SHORTER THAN THE LENGTH OF YOUR CUSHION

Layout and Construction

1 Measure your swing and make a custom pattern piece to these dimensions, adding one inch around all the edges. This gives you a ½-inch seam allowance and allows for the depth of your cushion. (This cushion has no boxing, so you don't need a lot of depth.) This pattern piece is the Top and Bottom of the cushion. Fold the tablecloth so you can center the pattern on its design elements. Cut out the pieces (figure 1).

Fig. 1   top and bottom   ------- **fold**

2 To add the zipper, stitch one long side of the Top and Bottom together, right sides facing, leaving an opening that's the appropriate size for your zipper. (For example, in this project, the length of the cushion is 34 inches, so I left an opening for a 28-inch zipper.) Center the zipper in the opening and use a zipper foot to stitch the zipper. Now, unzip the zipper.

3 Pin the Top and Bottom pieces together, right sides facing, and stitch all around the cushion. Clip the corners. Turn the cushion through the open zipper.

4 Add the batting, stuffing, or cushion to complete. If you use a foam cushion, you can wrap it with batting for extra comfort.

Terrific Tablecloth Shirt

This shirt and its variation elevate the tablecloth to high fashion. Look for checks or stripes for these blouses.

You Will Need
- BASIC SEWING SUPPLIES
- LARGE STRIPED TABLECLOTH
- 6 VINTAGE BUTTONS

Pattern
- VOGUE PATTERNS 1813

Pattern Pieces
- FRONT
- BACK
- YOKE BACK
- SLEEVE D
- COLLAR D
- POCKET

Pattern Alteration
Make this change while following the instructions in the pattern envelope:

Hem
I really like a shirttail hem, so I altered the hemline on the Front and Back. To get a curved hemline, draw a curve at the side corners of the Front and Back pattern pieces, as shown below. Allow ½ inch to turn the hem under.

Layout and Construction

1 Fold the tablecloth and arrange the pieces to take advantage of the stripes (figure 1). In this project, the stripes fall along the Sleeve, Pocket, and Collar, as well as the hem. Note how the intersection of the stripes accents the Front as shown in the photo on page 122. Cut out the pieces.

2 Follow the pattern's instructions for construction, noting the hem alteration listed at the left.

Tip: In a perfect world, you could lay out and construct this blouse in the simple way described above. Unfortunately, I didn't have enough of this fabric to cut out the whole sleeve, so I pieced it together to get the look I wanted; if you look closely, you can see the seam. Remember that you can always alter the pattern pieces to meet your fabric needs if you are creative enough!

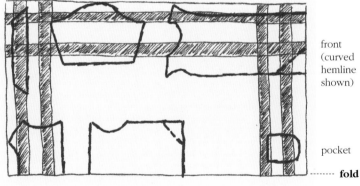

sleeve D

collar D

front (curved hemline shown)

pocket

fold

yoke back   back (curved hemline shown)
Fig. 1

Variation: Blue Checked Tablecloth Shirt

Pattern Alteration

Note the hem change listed on page 123 of this book while following the pattern's instructions.

Layout and Construction

1 Fold the tablecloth and place the Front, Sleeve, and Collar on the straight grain; put the Back and Yoke Back on the fold. Be sure to match the stripes at the side seams.

2 Follow the pattern's instructions for construction, noting the alteration listed on page 123. I omitted the pocket in this variation.

Tip: Another way you can be creative with your garments is to vary the number of buttons you use. In this checked variation, I used only four buttons, while I added six to the other blouse. If you happen to have only four great vintage buttons, but the pattern calls for six, simply adjust the spacing of the buttonholes.

Pattern Courtesy of The McCall Pattern Company: Vogue Patterns 1813

You Will Need
- BASIC SEWING SUPPLIES
- LARGE CHECKED TABLECLOTH
- 4 VINTAGE BUTTONS

Pattern
- VOGUE PATTERNS 1813

Pattern Pieces
- FRONT
- BACK
- YOKE BACK
- SLEEVE D
- COLLAR D

Reversible Wrap Skirt

Here's a fabulous way to use not one, but two, great
patterned linens. Reverse the skirt to suit your mood.

Reversible Wrap Skirt

You Will Need

- BASIC SEWING SUPPLIES
- 2 LARGE TABLECLOTHS, 1 WITH STRIPED BORDER
- 2 VINTAGE BUTTONS

Pattern

- DOS DE TEJAS PATTERNS: THE ULTIMATE WRAP SKIRT #5032

Pattern Pieces

- FRONT
- FRONT OVERLAY
- BACK
- TIE
- CUSTOM RIGHT TIE

Pattern Alterations

Make these changes while following the instructions in the pattern envelope:

Tie

I made the Right Tie a separate piece, because it hindered the placement of the skirt pieces on my vintage fabric. To change your pattern, too, cut the tie off of the Front Overlay (figure 1). You'll cut it out as a separate piece, adding a ½-inch seam allowance along the edge where you cut it from the Front Overlay. Add a corresponding seam allowance to the skirt. After you've cut out both pieces, stitch the Right Tie to the Front Overlay, right sides together.

Finishing

I used this method to place the buttonhole closure: Try on the skirt and tie it. Use a water-soluble marker to mark the buttonhole location on the opposite side of the Front Overlay from the Tie, near the side seam (figure 2). Reverse the skirt, tie it again, and check the placement of the buttonhole. Now, make the buttonhole and sew a button on the inside and the outside of the Front at the marked spot, so you can button it closed no matter which side you wear on the outside.

Layout and Construction

1 Lay the tablecloth flat. Place the Front, Front Overlay, Tie, and Right Tie as shown (figure 3). Remember to add a ½-inch seam allowance to the Right Tie and the Front Overlay where the pieces were cut from one another. Cut out each piece separately.

2 Fold the remaining tablecloth and cut out the Back on the fold (figure 4).

3 Cut the second skirt (the reversible skirt lining) out of another tablecloth, following the directions above.

4 Follow the pattern's instructions for construction, noting the alterations listed at the left.

Pattern Courtesy of Dos de Tejas Patterns, Designer L. Karen Odam: The Ultimate Wrap Skirt #5032

front overlay—cut off tie

Fig. 1

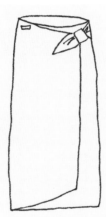

Fig. 2

left tie

front

right tie (cut from front overlay)

front overlay

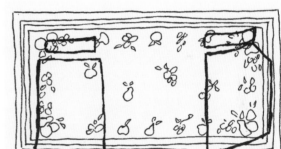

Fig. 3

back

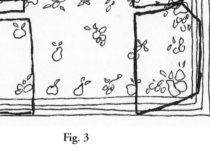

Fig. 4

fold

Fabric Gallery

To help you design and create your own project, here is a sampling of the fabrics I used in *Sewing with Fabulous Vintage Fabrics.* On the left are the original textiles, and on the right are the projects I made from them.

page 98

page 104

page 120

page 82

page 106

page 115

page 50

page 108

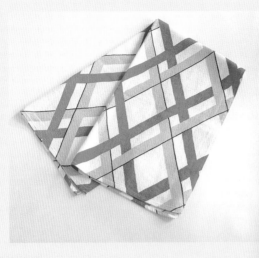

page 80

page 92

Metric Conversion Chart

Inches	Millimeters (mm) Centimeters (cm)	Inches	Millimeters (mm) Centimeters (cm)	Inches	Millimeters (mm) Centimeters (cm)
⅛	3 MM	8½	21.6 CM	23	58.4 CM
3/16	5 MM	9	22.9 CM	23½	59.7 CM
¼	6 MM	9½	24.1 CM	24	61 CM
5/16	8 MM	10	25.4 CM	24½	62.2 CM
⅜	9.5 MM	10½	26.7 CM	25	63.5 CM
7/16	1.1 CM	11	27.9 CM	25½	64.8 CM
½	1.3 CM	11½	29.2 CM	26	66 CM
9/16	1.4 CM	12	30.5 CM	26½	67.3 CM
⅝	1.6 CM	12½	31.8 CM	27	68.6 CM
11/16	1.7 CM	13	33 CM	27½	69.9 CM
¾	1.9 CM	13½	34.3 CM	28	71.1 CM
13/16	2.1 CM	14	35.6 CM	28½	72.4 CM
⅞	2.2 CM	14½	36.8 CM	29	73.7 CM
15/16	2.4 CM	15	38.1 CM	29½	74.9 CM
1	2.5 CM	15½	39.4 CM	30	76.2 CM
1½	3.8 CM	16	40.6 CM	30½	77.5 CM
2	5 CM	16½	41.9 CM	31	78.7 CM
2½	6.4 CM	17	43.2 CM	31½	80 CM
3	7.6 CM	17½	44.5 CM	32	81.3 CM
3½	8.9 CM	18	45.7 CM	32½	82.6 CM
4	10.2 CM	18½	47 CM	33	83.8 CM
4½	11.4 CM	19	48.3 CM	33½	85 CM
5	12.7 CM	19½	49.5 CM	34	86.4 CM
5½	14 CM	20	50.8 CM	34½	87.6 CM
6	15.2 CM	20½	52 CM	35	88.9 CM
6½	16.5 CM	21	53.3 CM	35½	90.2 CM
7	17.8 CM	21½	54.6 CM	36	91.4 CM
7½	19 CM	22	55 CM		
8	20.3 CM	22½	57.2 CM		

Pattern Credits

THE CHILDREN'S CORNER PATTERNS

3814 Cleghorn Avenue
P.O. Box 150161
Nashville, Tennessee 37215
800-543-6915
www.childrenscornerfabric.com

*Grace (pages 72, 74, 76); Handsewing 1 (30)
(Gown) (pages 60, 64); Hillary (pages 38, 40,
42); Louise (pages 100, 102)*

DOS DE TEJAS PATTERNS

P.O. Box 1636
Sherman, Texas 75091
800-883-5278
www.dosdetejas.com

The Ultimate Wrap Skirt #5032 (page 125)

THE McCALL PATTERN COMPANY

P.O. Box 3755
Manhattan, Kansas 66505-3755
United States: 800-766-3619, extension 488
International: 785-776-4041, extension 488
Projects are made with McCall's and Vogue patterns. For a complete selection of our patterns, please visit your local retail fabric store or visit our website at www.mccallpattern.com.

*McCalls: 2991 (page 80); 3501 (page 104);
4073 (page 108)*

*Vogue: 1813 (pages 122, 124); 2105 (page 78);
2491 (pages 112, 114); 2730 (pages 66, 68);
7628 (pages 85, 87); 7726 (page 92)*

CUTTING LINE DESIGNS

900 S. Orlando Ave.
Winter Park, Florida 32789
877-734-5818
www.fabriccollections.com

*By Popular Demand #60565
(pages 32, 34, 70)*

THE SEWING WORKSHOP

2010 Balboa Street
San Francisco, California 94121
800-466-1599
www.sewingworkshop.com

*Chopin Blouse (pages 53, 56, 58);
San Diego Jacket (page 88)*

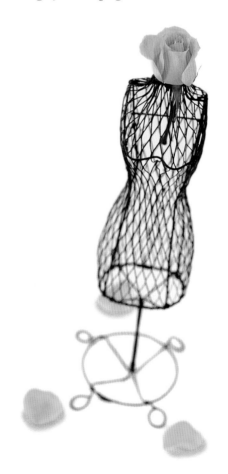

Acknowledgments

Thank you to all of my friends who were willing to read the rough drafts of this book and offer input and suggestions, especially Mary and John Huff. Thanks so much to the illustrator, Jennifer D. Wallace, for lending her personality to the drawings and for being my confidant throughout the entire process of producing the book.

Soline Donatiu of French Options and Megan Kirby were gracious hosts for the location photography, and Sandra Stambaugh created the beautiful images. Models Mary Casey, Tanayha Faison, Margaret Murphy, and Jasmine Villarreal looked lovely in the garments. Megan Kirby also generously donated fabric for some of the projects in this book, as did Terry Taylor. Thank you to the professionals at Lark Books, who brought the book to life.

Index

A Note About Suppliers

Usually, the supplies you need for making the projects in Lark books can be found at your local craft supply store, discount mart, home improvement center, or retail shop relevant to the topic of the book. Occasionally, however, you may need to buy materials or tools from specialty suppliers. In order to provide you with the most up-to-date information, we have created a list of suppliers on our Web site, which we update on a regular basis. Visit us at www.larkbooks.com, click on "Craft Supply Sources," and then click on the relevant topic. You will find numerous companies listed with their web address and/or mailing address and phone number.